'Our secular Western age assumes that life's pri... feel good. Here we are reminded that the Christian's purpose for living is not to feel good but, by God's grace, to become good, to be godly. And Christ-likeness only occurs when we take up our cross and follow him. This is more than a primer for graduating students seeking to count the cost for overseas missions. It's a book that reminds all Christians of the cost and high privilege of true discipleship. I recommend it highly!'

Rebecca Manley Pippert, author of *Out of the Saltshaker*

'Deeply moving. A timely and refreshing reminder of the costs and privileges of serving Christ in other cultures. Some of the testimonies in this book are disturbing and challenging. These people have been moved by the conviction that the gospel is the greatest message in the history of the world. As you read, you too will be challenged to contribute to the great and glorious task of taking that message to the ends of the earth.'

Lindsay Brown, General Secretary IFES

'Here is the antidote to the deadly lie that getting my own way is what is best for me. Here is God's call to liberating, costly obedience, even unto…, in the full knowledge that Jesus is with us even unto.… *My Rights? My God?* is an honest, compassionate and uncompromisingly biblical examination of the struggle to say "no" to self and "yes" to God.'

Don Cormack, author of *Killing Fields, Living Fields*

'There is an urgent need to heed the message of this book. It convincingly presents key biblical emphases which have been neglected by the Church, influenced as it is by the culture of our day. I believe that churches in affluent countries which neglect it stand the risk of disqualifying themselves from being missionary sending churches.'

Ajith Fernando, Director of Youth for Christ, Sri Lanka

'Robin Wells exudes the joy, and shares the pain, of Jesus' promise to those who leave "home or brothers or sisters or mother or father or children or fields for me and the gospel" (Mark 10:29). The stories of missionaries receiving "a hundred times as much" as they left behind, and of the persecutions they face (Mark 10:30), are fresh and contemporary. Anyone tempted to hold on to the "right to a normal life" will benefit from this portrayal of the "joy of sacrifice" in response to the call of our loving God.'

Steve Hayner, President, InterVarsity Christian Fellowship, USA

'This gripping book is a manifesto for Christians who are willing to rebel against our myopic, me-first culture. It gives us Bible realism and real-life stories for people who want to get serious about life, about mission, about living for Jesus. Always facing up to practical issues, it shows the way towards the "joy of sacrifice".'

Keith Walker, World Missions Co-ordinator, UCCF

'The author highlights some of the toughest challenges as well as the deepest privileges experienced by many who serve Christ far from home. For anyone considering cross-cultural mission — prepare to be challenged!'

Lesley Bilinda, All Nations Christian College, and author of *The Colour of Darkness*

my rights?
my GOD?

robin wells

MONARCH
BOOKS

emis

First published under the title *My Rights. My God.* by
Monarch Books in the UK in 2000, Concorde House,
Grenville Place, Mill Hill, London NW7 3SA.

Reissued as *My Rights? My God?* in 2001.

First published by Monarch Books in the USA in 2001.

Cover design by Kregel Publications
Illustrations by Taffy Davies

Distributed by:
UK: STL, PO Box 300, Kingstown Broadway,
Carlisle, Cumbria CA3 0QS;
USA: Kregel Publications, PO Box 2607,
Grand Rapids, Michigan 49501.

ISBN 1 85424 556 2 (UK)
ISBN 0 8254 6024 7 (USA)

British Library Cataloguing Data
A catalogue record for this book is available from the
British Library.

emis

Published in conjunction with EMIS, Billy Graham Center, Wheaton
College, Wheaton, Illinois 60187-5593, USA

Book design and production for the publisher by
Gazelle Creative Productions,
Concorde House, Grenville Place, Mill Hill,
London NW7 3SA.

About the author

Robin Wells is South African. He studied Chemistry at the University of Pretoria, and then gained his doctorate from Imperial College, London. Robin has been active in student ministry in South Africa, and more widely as a member of the Executive Committee of the International Fellowship of Evangelical Students (IFES); he served as General Secretary of the Universities and Colleges Christian Fellowship (UCCF), its UK movement, for twelve years. More recently his work with the Africa Evangelical Fellowship and SIM has included the selection and training of missionaries.

For Val

▶ Contents

Acknowledgements

First, I must thank those people whose stories illustrate this book. It was a humbling privilege to work with them. Some stories have to be anonymous, but there is One who says, 'I know your afflictions and your poverty – yet you are rich!' A word of appreciation, too, to those who sent me material which in the end I did not use.

Then I am also indebted to several people who read all or part of the manuscript or made helpful comments and suggestions to spur the project on, notably Bill Fietje, Barb Rahn, Bill Barnett, Sam Allberry, Katy Bingham, Gwyneth James, Bethan Parmenter, Nigel Head and Allie Schwaar; to Roger Chouler for his excellent book design; and to Carole Parker for her painstaking work in compiling the appendices.

My thanks go to Julia Cameron of OMF International for her role as critical and encouraging editor, and to Tony Collins of Monarch Books for his contribution to the shaping and development of the book and to David Miller of FEBA/FEBC for producing the CD. A special word of thanks goes to my wife for her forbearance and encouragement during the writing process. Thanks, too, to my SIM colleagues for their tolerance and goodwill.

Finally, I wish to pay tribute to Mabel Williamson, whose *Have We No Rights?* was a help and inspiration to four decades of young people facing the same tough realities of service abroad which I address here.

Foreword

Robin Wells has a track record as one of God's marathon runners. I hope that many potential runners for the Kingdom will let these pages help them get into the race and stay in it.

This unique and important book is especially needed today when everyone is bombarded with postmodern culture. It is hardly surprising that people grow up to distrust authority and to celebrate autonomy. Our easy lifestyles and high disposable incomes make it all the harder to keep gospel priorities at the front of our thinking. Robin's analysis of the 'cultures of comfort' needs to be taken to heart. I believe *My Rights? My God?* helps us find a glorious and biblical path through the confusion and darkness of the Western mindset. This powerful message on the Lordship of Christ should impact every aspect of our lives.

In short, here is a well thought out and compelling presentation. Let's not ignore it. It is especially relevant to those who want to spend their lives in cross-cultural ministry, but it is more than that. It is a valuable and needed message for *every one* of us.

It is my prayer that people will not only read and study this book, but will take it seriously enough to play a part in getting it out to others – not only in their own country, but across the globe. I long for God's people to realise afresh the power of the printed page, and to become more committed in their reading and distribution of books like this.

George Verwer

Start here

This book is for anyone who wants to read it, but it is especially for those who still have most of their lives ahead of them, and who may be facing big decisions about their future... for any who are asking if God might be calling them to serve him in another culture, and who are facing the implications of that.

> Jesus doesn't call us to impulsive or unthinking action. There are big issues at stake. There are real costs.

If that is where you are, perhaps you already realise that such a call can be costly. You may have friends who have taken that path, and you may have seen something of what it has meant for them – financial or career sacrifices, separation from family and friends, and so on. The purpose of this book is to explore these costs, and to look at them in the light of the Bible.

We need to be realistic. We should carefully count the cost of Christian discipleship, whatever the path we take. Jesus doesn't call us to impulsive or unthinking action but to look at the pros and cons with open eyes. There are big issues at stake. There are real costs. But if we are serious about following Christ, there can be no doubt about the bottom line: putting him first always gives the best outcome.

My Rights...

These issues raise serious questions for those who live in the West or in countries with comparable standards of living: people from the 'cultures of comfort'. In the ease and affluence of our lives, making sacrifices can seem unreasonable. The world we live in whispers in our ears that we are entitled to hold on to every comfort – that we have a right to do so. Christians, like everyone else, breathe in this atmosphere and need to be aware that this is happening. We cannot be immune to the influences around us. So we need always to be letting the Bible interrogate our world, and also our own personal patterns of belief and behaviour.

> We need to let the Bible interrogate our world

Protecting our rights has been a strong theme in the Western world through the past three or four generations. We see it emerge in all sorts of ways. In political conflicts. In debates on gender issues. In questions thrown up by medical progress. But how godly a theme is it? Any one of these areas can create a mindset that jealously protects our 'rights' against God's authority, and shields us against any calling to make sacrifices; a mindset that challenges Christ's lordship in our lives.

...My God

So why should you follow a costly path – if that's the way God is calling you? What right have I to encourage you in that? Well, I have no right, but I have a responsibility. You and I stand together under the authority of the Bible, and of the Lord of whom the Bible speaks. And that brings on us a responsibility to help each other in our discipleship and in our obedience to the Scriptures.

This Lord of whom the Bible speaks is the Lord Jesus whose cross is at the centre of our faith. I was struck recently by this remark: 'We will take sacrifice seriously only if we understand the cross.' When Jesus taught his disciples that he would have to die on the cross, he gave them the cross as a pattern for their discipleship. (See, for example, Mark 8:31-38.) Christians, then, bear the imprint of the cross on their lives. So we should not be surprised if the Christian life calls for some toughness: he told us it would.

Christians bear the imprint of the cross on their lives

Now let's turn to the last meal Jesus had with his inner circle of friends before his death. He taught them that, in his death, his body was being given for them. 'This is my body,' he said, 'given for you.' So as we take part in the Lord's supper or Communion service, we are helped to see ourselves, as individuals, needing his death for us. 'He loved me and gave himself for me,' said Paul.

But in Mark's account, we have a second emphasis alongside that. Jesus gives his disciples the shared cup of wine with these words: 'This is my blood of the covenant, which is poured out for many' (Mark 14:24). Not only for them, but 'for *many*'. In the intense privacy of that upper room he directs their thoughts outwards, to the waiting world. They are to think not only of their own needs but also of the world into which he is sending them. Mission is of the essence of the gospel.

* * *

As we go through the book we'll meet a number of people who have already faced the questions of cost. We'll learn how they view them. I have talked to a wide range of people with experience of different continents. Most are still fairly young. There are things to be learned from those with greater experience, of course, and their stories come in too. In addition to these, some of the quotations I have used are 'classics'.

People have urged me, again and again, not to let realism about hardships overshadow the joys and satisfaction of serving God in costly paths. Talk of the 'joy of sacrifice,' they said. And I note that they are people who have been through a good deal of suffering in their own lives.

> If you really want to do business with God over your future, do it

If, when you have finished this book, you really want to do business with God over your future, do it. Don't let the attractions of the career package – or anything else – crowd out what God may be saying to you. To help you in this, I have included a reading list at the back, and there is a host of websites to browse. Those of us who have worked on putting this book together will be praying that God would be at work in the lives of its readers. Whatever you do with your future, may it bring him glory.

My Rights? My God?

If you want to do business with God
over your future, do it.

The Myths of Mission

▌ 'Christian work is for people who can't get into the career they want.'

▌ 'Everyone who wants to share their faith should be a pastor or a missionary.'

▌ 'You have to be stinking rich to go on summer programmes.'

▌ 'Being interested in world mission is for fanatics, not for the rest of us.'

▌ 'If you have a good skill, you shouldn't waste it overseas.'

▌ 'If you're *really* converted, you won't go into business. You'll be a full-time evangelist.'

▌ 'Mission damages people's culture.'

▌ 'We have no right to tell people that they should believe in Christ.'

▌ 'Mission is only for single people.'

My Rights? My God?

▶ Chapter 1

Cultures of comfort

T here is a wonderful honesty and realism in the Bible. It offers us no escapism. It doesn't try to trick us into any action by hiding the consequences from us. Jesus himself warns us that the Christian life is costly: following him is no easy option. In fact, Jesus explicitly calls us to take stock of our lives and weigh up the cost of discipleship. He tells us that anyone who wants to be his disciple 'must deny himself and take up his cross and follow' him (Matthew 16:24).

> The Bible offers us no escapism

All discipleship is costly. But some people are called to a costlier path than others, and serving overseas can be one example of this. It is a myth, by the way, that a tough and sacrificial lifestyle is easier for missionaries than it would be for others, just because God has called them to it. They are made no differently from us and feel suffering as much. The pain is as real for them as it would be for anybody.

So why should anyone take that path? Why should we give up the prospect of a decent house, a nice car, a good salary, and a benefits package that will see us into an early retirement full of good holidays? Why not stay in our own country and make a name for ourselves in our profession? After all, no role is wrong in itself. We can please God in any legitimate occupation. There is no sense in which it is a 'more spiritual' calling to work overseas, and there are situations in our own country where it can be very tough to be a Christian. And the voice saying these things in our ears, distracting us from our high calling, is reinforced by the world we live in.

> There are situations in our own country where it can be very tough to be a Christian

Amusing ourselves to death

We in the West live in a very comfortable world. And we keep on expecting ever more comfort and convenience. We can usually find quick relief from pain when we are ill or have an accident. Many previously life-threatening conditions are now almost trivial, thanks to medical advances. Just think back to what life was like for our great-grandparents before the discovery of anaesthetics or even antibiotics. How different our world is from theirs.

The wealthy and inventive cultures in the West have produced any number of ways for us to amuse and entertain ourselves, and it is no longer just the rich who can afford them. That is the case whether we like going on energetic skiing holidays or prefer to settle for the physically less demanding option of the Sega *Dreamcast*. No surprise, then, that Neil Postman, Professor of Communication Arts and Sciences at New York University, should entitle his reflection on our culture *Amusing Ourselves to Death*.

The 20th-century Christian philosopher Francis Schaeffer coined the term 'personal peace and affluence' to describe what drives human aspirations in the postmodern world. This was most perceptive. Without conscious thought, we drift towards that, and away from service which is costly. Let's recognise this bias in ourselves, and be aware of the dangers. It stems from a self-fulfilling and self-

My Rights? My God?

Amusing ourselves to death

19

indulgent mindset, in which the aim is far removed from pleasing God.

We are living in a world which has anaesthetised itself to horror and tragedy. We can still say 'What a pity, those poor people', but our emotions are left intact. The upbeat music at the end of the news bulletin has pulled us back into what we are beguiled into thinking is 'reality'. We enjoy the comfort of an armchair thousands of miles from the area of conflict, the drought, or the plane crash. We might as well have been hearing news of another world, another planet. Our own comfort zone has not been invaded, and we have looked on as voyeurs, entertained by the plight of fellow human beings for whom Christ died.

> We look on as voyeurs, entertained by the plight of people for whom Christ died

If we look at things in the sweep of human history, we should note that our prosperous and comfortable world is most unusual. No one in any culture or with whatever riches has ever lived as comfortably as we do now. The comparative freedom from wars that impinge on us and on our families and friends is also an unusual blip in history. We have grown up in a war-free comfort zone, and have come to take it for granted. We assume it is the norm. Yes, there are conflicts, famines, floods, droughts and other natural disasters in far-off places. But these are all mediated through television reports or through newspapers. They do not really touch our lives.

In no way is the West of the last few generations typical of human history. If we build our lives, and our views of the world, on the belief that it is, we are building on sand. If we assume we have the right to such a lifestyle we fly in the face of world realities.

History also shows us that no one – not even the privileged few – can entirely escape pain or disappointment.

These things are part of the human predicament. In spite of all that has been opened up to us through our education, and through medical and technological progress, we know frustration, pain and death, and there is nothing we can do to avoid them. What's wrong? Why, when we are created with desires and the capacity for pleasure, is there this sense of futility in the world?

This is a key question. And as with so many issues which touch on what it means to be human, we find ourselves needing to look back to the story of creation to explore it. Can we find a framework that makes sense of our desires for pleasure and also makes sense of the need at times to say 'No' to legitimate aspirations?

Where it all went wrong

We need to start the story where the story starts, with God's creation of a world that he described as 'very good'. We can't understand exactly what that 'very good' world was like, but it is clear that it was very different from the world we live in. It, and all beings in it, perfectly fulfilled the roles they were created for, and reflected the glory of God. What a world! Then swiftly the scene changes, and in Genesis chapter 3 the Bible turns our attention to a darker picture.

The first man and woman, created with a capacity for pleasure but also accountable to their Creator, are seduced into an act of rebellion which theologians call 'the Fall'. It was to leave the whole human race with many scars. Were it not for this event in our history, this book would not be written. There would be no need for Christian witness, for the whole world would be in fellowship with God as Creator. There is a sense in which all of human experience finds this chapter of Genesis as its reference point. For a true understanding of what it is to be human and of why we need salvation, it is the key.

One outcome of 'the Fall' is that we always seem dissatisfied. We end up hoping for things that cannot fulfil their promise. Another result is that our desire for what is good becomes distorted: the things we long for do not reflect a longing for perfect harmony between child and heavenly Father, but instead express defiance and resentment. We desire what *we* want, and we no longer desire only what he wants. The rebellion recounted in Genesis chapter 3 aimed to place us on the throne that is rightfully God's. As a result of this, we are born as fallen human beings, and with a mistaken sense that it is our 'right' to satisfy our desires.

This is universal, of course, but it is particularly noticeable in the West. We believe we have rights to unlimited comfort and safety, and we look for someone to blame when things go wrong.

> We believe we have rights to unlimited comfort and safety

There are good and legitimate uses of the word 'rights', but more often than not it is used in defiance of authority, and particularly of God's authority. When through Adam's sin we became rebels, we all fell under God's judgment and we all forfeited our rights. The language of 'rights' can become the language of rebellion against God. It often is just that.

> The language of 'rights' can become the language of rebellion against God

What of the Christian? Do we share in the futility that grips the human race? The answer is both yes and no. God's plan of redemption is full and perfect. We have a certain hope of a new creation – including us – that will be perfect in every respect, free from all disappointment and discomfort. But that is in the future. We can't expect full satisfaction now. In the meantime we share in the pains and imperfections of life, but with a perspective that transforms it all.

Getting things in perspective

As I have talked with the people whose stories are in this book, I have been repeatedly struck by one thing. They show no self-pity, nor any regret for having obeyed Christ. Why is this? I sat at a meal in Cochabamba, Bolivia, with a number of SIM missionaries, and we talked around these things. 'The issue is perspective,' said one American missionary.

The issue is perspective

There is a great biblical principle in that. We see the principle in the examples of Jesus himself and the apostle Paul. They didn't look at their sufferings in isolation. They put them in perspective alongside other things; they made comparisons. Listen to how it is put in the letter to the Hebrews: 'Let us fix our eyes on Jesus… who for the joy set before him endured the cross, scorning the shame' (Hebrews 12:2). He put the suffering of the cross alongside the miracle of all that the cross would accomplish, and doing this enabled him to 'scorn' its pain.

Paul, too, suffered for his faith, and like his master he was able to put it in perspective. At the end of a passage in which he gives an appalling description of his sufferings, he writes: 'Our light and momentary troubles are achieving for us an eternal glory that far outweighs them all. So we fix our eyes not on what is seen, but on what is unseen. For what is seen is temporary, but what is unseen is eternal' (2 Corinthians 4:7,18). Paul didn't deny the reality of his sufferings, but he was able to see them as 'light and momentary' in comparison with unseen but eternal realities.

A recent example. I was talking to a young missionary whose experiences are recounted in these chapters. He and his wife and children have just begun their second term of service in the Philippines, in a tough situation. I asked him what had kept them there when the going got tough. No doubt with the parable of the talents in mind (see Matthew 25:14ff), he responded, 'I didn't want to miss the "Well done."' He had the perspective!

> 'I didn't want to miss the "Well done."'

This view of hardships makes sense of the passages in the New Testament that call us to rejoice in sufferings. It is no perverted masochism, enjoying pain for its own sake. It is a triumph of perspective. Take Jesus' own words to his followers: 'Blessed are you when people insult you, persecute you and falsely say all kinds of evil against you because of me. Rejoice and be glad, because great is your reward in heaven' (Matthew 5:11,12).

So Paul writes, 'We rejoice in our sufferings' (Romans 5:3); he can do this because of the results he sees flowing into people's lives through those sufferings. He goes on: 'suffering produces perseverance, perseverance character, and character hope.' In turn, James urges: 'Consider it pure joy, my brothers, whenever you face trials of many kinds' (James 1:2). His reasons? 'The testing of your faith develops perseverance. Perseverance must finish its work so that you may be mature and complete, not lacking anything.'

A final example of perspective, this time from C T Studd, the famous 19th century sportsman and missionary: 'If Jesus Christ be God, and if he died for me, then nothing is too great for me to do for him.'

Getting real

These are not examples of mindless fanaticism. They are calls to use our minds and make serious comparisons. This book is a serious call to look at the 'bottom line'. Is the 'bottom line' to be seen entirely in financial terms, and in the benefits money can buy us and our families? A mortgage paid off in time for early retirement? A good school for our children?

If we know our God, and we want to make it our aim to please him, our horizons will be further away. We will look to things that are unseen. For some of us there *will* be a comfortable lifestyle, but we shall hold it lightly, and as a trust from God. For others of us, we shall be finding out what Christ meant by the 'hundred times' return he promised to those who give up homes and families for his sake (see Matthew 19:29).

> Finding out what Christ meant by the 'hundred times' return he promised

Recommended reading

George Verwer, *Out of Your Comfort Zone* (OM Publishing)
Michael Griffiths, *Take My Life* (OM Publishing)
Bruce Milne, *Know the Truth: A Handbook of Christian Belief* (IVP)
John Piper, *Let the Nations Be Glad!: The Supremacy of God in Missions* (Baker Book House)

My thoughts

My Rights? My God?

Lloyd's story

Lloyd was an MK ('missionary kid'), or what is known now as a 'third-culture' child. He grew up in Kashmir in India and his family moved back to Australia when he was eleven. He qualified as a Quantity Surveyor and landed a great job. He loved his work. But only a few months after his final exams, he felt the Lord was leading him to Eastern Europe to serve short-term with Operation Mobilisation.

Lloyd remembers opening his Bible at Hebrews chapter 11. 'I was challenged by Abraham's story. He was called and obeyed, not knowing where he was going. (Hebrews 11:8). It was as if I had a choice to stay back – or step out. And I stepped out, not knowing then what it would mean. I have never regretted it.' Obedience had a cost, however: he'd just bought his own apartment in Perth, he had a secure job, and he loved his surfy car!

As the months in Eastern Europe passed, Lloyd knew he had to think about the future.

'The time in Siberia was exciting – people were being saved, a church was planted. The whole week was a round of Russian Bible studies and prayer meetings, and street evangelism! But through all this I still didn't know if God wanted me to stay there. Part of me was drawn by the thought of going back to Perth and pursuing a lucrative career. But I kept thinking of Hebrews 11, and wondered what I was aiming for. What was God's best?'

One hard question had been the issue of church support. Although his church had supported him in prayer, they hadn't stood behind him financially. How would he survive more years in mission without that support?

'During this amazing time in Siberia, the economy in Australia went through a shaky patch. Interest rates went up and rents fell. Back home my parents were watching my bank balance dwindle with not enough rent coming in to cover the outgoings. The flat was finally sold at a greatly reduced price and instead of an asset and a bank balance, I suddenly had a debt of $8,000. It was hard to lose that security and what I had worked for over several years.'

Still reeling from the news, Lloyd was wondering, 'What on earth do I do now, Lord?' Then God spoke to him again through Hebrews chapter 11, and Moses' choice to follow the Lord. So Lloyd decided that he would go home, work to pay off the debt – and then come back to his beloved Russia. Soon after he decided this, his church wrote to say they'd like to start supporting him financially!

In some ways that period looked like a costly two years. Lloyd lost his own home and 'secure' future, gaining instead

My Rights? My God?

a debt, and longer term, a call to a deeply unstable country. But he also saw how the Lord walked through this time with him. And he has now been able to pay off his debts and return to Russia.

That was in the early 1990s. Lloyd is still in Russia, and now married to Katherine, whose degree in English from Cambridge also turned out to be the launching pad for ministry in Eastern Europe with OM. I could go on to tell of her call to mission as she watched the Berlin Wall come down; of the way she then stayed back in the UK to nurse her dying grandmother; and of her joy in being part of the first evangelistic outreach in Albania for nearly half a century when people clamoured to hear the gospel. Lloyd and Katherine have now moved to St Petersburg and Lloyd is the Field Leader for OM in Russia. There are plenty of challenges still each day for both of them – but God remains faithful to those he has called.

> ▶ Chapter 2

Money and standards of living

Life in Oz can be great for a young man with a good education and a good job. That was Lloyd's experience before God called him to move into another culture. His story touches on one of the obvious costs of serving abroad – money! Moving to live in another culture often brings with it a lowered standard of living, especially if we're going to be working with a Christian agency such as a missionary society. Taking the plunge and accepting a drop in living standards is one thing. Working through the issues when we face them in the first months abroad is another. Seeing our contemporaries enjoying increasing prosperity is yet another!

The wealthy West

Until we've been in contact with two-thirds-world poverty, we easily fail to grasp the gulf between the world's 'haves' and 'have-nots'. We may know in theory that a lot of the world is less affluent than we are, but often it doesn't sink in until we see it for ourselves.

Let us at least note the facts in passing. The table below shows the Gross National Product (GNP) per capita of several countries, both Western and 'two-thirds-world'. Now of course these are just the bare figures. To make valid comparisons you need to take all sorts of factors into account. But such extremes must mean something! There is obviously the most enormous difference between what we take for granted in Europe and North America, on the one hand, and how men and women live in much of the rest of the world. We enjoy an affluence way beyond the imagining of millions of our fellow human beings.

GNP measured at Purchasing Power Parity

Country	GNP per capita (Dollars 1998)
Malawi	730
Mozambique	850
Nigeria	820
Pakistan	1,560
Rwanda	690
Switzerland	26,620
United Kingdom	20,640
United States	29,340

Figures (for 1998) from the World Bank's Annual World Development Report

It's worth putting any puny sacrifices we might make against that backdrop. It's also useful to remember that, while many live in the most appalling and tragic poverty in the world, there are also millions who live full and rewarding lives on a fraction of the incomes we expect in the West. 'Needs' can be relative, and what we regard as needs may well be unimaginable luxury to others.

Millions live full lives on a fraction of the incomes we expect

How far will my living standards drop?

These world realities mean that some adjustment of lifestyle shouldn't surprise us. If we are going abroad to take up a normal professional job, it may be possible to live about as comfortably as we do at home, depending on the country. But in many places the conditions simply will not allow for the same comforts and conveniences. (See some of Marty Bell's comments at the beginning of the next chapter.) There won't be a Next or a Macy's down the road. You won't have a choice of TV channels. People may never have heard of your favourite food. And in less trivial ways you will be aware that you're not at home. Some places are primitive, and some are tough. There's no escaping that. Life won't be the same. That can be exciting too, of course.

You may be weighing up the possibility of going overseas with a mission or some other Christian agency. If so, it won't have escaped your attention that your expected income is unlikely to place you in the annual lists of the top 200 earners! You'll be facing the reality of a reduced income, lower – sometimes much lower – than you might take for granted in your home country. If it is paid in sterling or dollars, it may translate quite well into the soft currencies of a two-thirds-world country. But you will not have an employer paying a percentage of your salary into a pension fund, as most graduates in secular employment now expect. (Most mission agencies do make pension provision, but it will not compare with the pension some of your contemporaries will eventually be drawing.)

There is something else to take into account. The standard of living that we can maintain on our missionary allowance may still leave a great gap between us and those around us in our host country. Even missionaries may

> Your expected income is unlikely to place you in the top 200 earners

Dream on!

appear wealthy to most nationals! This raises some tough questions for us, if we want to have genuine friendships with Christians around us and want our ministry to be effective. If we are working alongside Christian nationals, how do we express our fellowship? As a rule, they will not expect us to live completely at their level. That is usually unwise and often impossible. But how great a discrepancy can our ministry tolerate?

Do we need to deny ourselves things to go some way towards bridging the gulf between what we can afford and how the people we work amongst live? These are agonising questions, and questions that may not have one absolutely right answer. But we should note the concern, and the fact that some of the most sensitive missionaries believe these are questions that we will need to answer. Once again we find ourselves battling with the issue of 'rights'. Is it not my right to live comfortably, enjoying the rewards my gifts, training and experience can receive?

Four ways money works

Let's look at some of the ways in which money 'works' in our culture. These may help identify the questions we will need to work through.

I **An indicator of how we are valued.** In our Western cultures money is widely seen as an indicator of how we are valued in our jobs. This is not necessarily wrong, and in fact it has been a feature of all cash economies, reaching back into biblical times. So increased output, greater responsibilities or greater risk-taking are rewarded with more money. While some people dislike this pattern, alternatives don't seem to work very well. Generally speaking, this is the way things function in our secular working environments.

It takes a mental shift of gear to get out of this mindset, and working for most donation-supported organisations will call for such a shift in thinking. We soon come to understand that in such organisations we do not get what we or others think we might deserve. Seniority may or may not be recognised with an increased salary or allowance, but in cases where it is, it is unlikely to be a significant 'jump', and will not equate with similar levels of responsibility in the business world or in the public sector. Merit and 'rights' don't come into it! Money is given to the mission for its ministry, and there is usually not enough to make the most of the opportunities. Accepting this way of thinking about money is one of the costs to be faced.

> Responsibility may not be recognised with an increased salary

| **A measure of success.** For some people it is *making* money that is the challenge. For them, it is not money itself that is the lure, or what money can buy, but simply the drive to succeed. So money-making becomes the measure of their success in running their business. It's like winning a game. These people usually play Monopoly with the same vigour, and often win! Money, for them, is more a matter of fascination than of covetousness.

Here again, we aren't looking at something that is evil in itself. There are many legitimate fascinations in life. But there are dangers. These things can become obsessive, and any obsession has its dangers. In advising the Corinthian Church about the uncertainties of their times, Paul uses an interesting word. He writes:

> Any obsession has its dangers

> What I mean, brothers, is that the time is short. From now on those who have wives should live as if they had none; those who mourn, as if they did not; those

My Rights? My God?

who are happy, as if they were not; those who buy something, as if it were not theirs to keep; those who use the things of the world, as if not engrossed in them.

(1 Corinthians 7:29-31)

The word translated 'engrossed' means something like 'over-using'. Paul is saying that there is a legitimate involvement with 'the things of this world', but that we can become preoccupied with them. They can loom too large in our thinking and compete with our commitment to other values and other loyalties.

| **A route to status symbols.** Money is a key to all sorts of status symbols, pleasures and recreations. It's what money can *buy* that is the lure. Some of these can be legitimate; for the Christian, some are a snare. Jesus warns against the dangerous distraction that we can find in 'worries, riches and pleasures' (Luke 8:14). They can stifle the work of God's Word in our lives. And we find that, when our mind is so filled with these things, we never have enough. However wealthy we are, and however easily we can buy what we want, we want more.

The Christian life is not a call to asceticism. God gives most of us more than we need, and to some of us he entrusts a great deal. Money can be put to good uses, and God calls some to earn big salaries and give to mission – George Verwer refers to such people as the 'unsung heroes'! How else would God's work be supported? Paul – like his master – never condemns wealth as such, nor does he teach us that all Christians should dispose of all their possessions. But he does warn of the dangers of wealth.

> God calls some to earn big salaries and give to mission

Paul writes to Timothy: 'People who want to get rich fall into temptation and a trap and into many foolish and harmful desires that plunge men into ruin and destruction. The love of money is a root of all kinds of evil. Some people, eager for money, have wandered from the faith and pierced themselves with many griefs.' (1 Timothy 6:9,10.) A staggering statement! But note his choice of words: '... *want to* get rich... *love of* money... *eager for* money'. He is warning against the desire for money, not its possession. A poor man who dreams of wealth may be more in view here than a rich man who is not a prisoner to his wealth.

Later in the same letter, Paul has a word for those who are wealthy. Timothy is to 'command those who are rich in this present world not to be arrogant nor to put their hope in wealth, which is so uncertain, but to put their hope in God, who richly provides us with everything for our enjoyment. Command them to do good, to be rich in good deeds, and to be generous and willing to share' (1 Timothy 6:17,18). Here again it is the wrong attitude to wealth that he warns against, and its selfish use.

| **A key to security.** The fourth way in which money functions in our cultures is for security. We earn money to provide food, shelter, clothing, holidays, children's education. We look ahead to retirement and make provision for a time when we will no longer be able to earn. Unemployment creates anxiety because we fear we may not be able to meet our needs and those of our family.

For some people thinking of going overseas, this is one of the big battles. Will they have enough? Will their family and children be adequately provided for? Our parents can go through the same struggles, whether they are Christians or not. Grandparents can be very

My Rights? My God?

anxious about their grandchildren! And that is understandable. It is natural – and good – to feel a sense of responsibility for the wellbeing of our families.

Perhaps security is the most sensitive of the roles that money plays, and one we need to explore further.

> Perhaps security is the most sensitive role money plays

Money and security

What is the Bible's perspective on security? Note the words of Paul quoted above: 'wealth is uncertain'. Look at Lloyd's story again, at the start of this chapter. He made what he thought was careful and adequate provision, but unforeseen changes in the economy landed him in debt. The financial future was not as sure and predictable as he had thought. And life is full of stories like that. This isn't to say that we shouldn't be prudent in planning our finances. I believe we should. But our ultimate security isn't to be found in our bank balance or our pension plans.

The other side of the equation is that, while wealth may be uncertain, God's care is certain. Jesus leaves us in no doubt about that in this striking passage from the Sermon on the Mount:

> Do not store up for yourselves treasures on earth, where moth and rust destroy, and where thieves break in and steal. But store up for yourselves treasures in heaven, where moth and rust do not destroy, and where thieves do not break in and steal. For where your treasure is, there your heart will be also.
> Therefore I tell you, do not worry about your life, what you will eat or drink; or about your body, what you will wear. Is not life more important than food, and the body more important than clothes? Look at the birds of the air; they do not sow or reap or store away in barns, and yet your heavenly Father feeds them. Are you not much more

valuable than they? Who of you by worrying can add a single hour to his life? And why do you worry about clothes? See how the lilies of the field grow. They do not labour or spin. Yet I tell you that not even Solomon in all his splendour was dressed like one of these. If that is how God clothes the grass of the field, which is here today and tomorrow is thrown into the fire, will he not much more clothe you, O you of little faith? So do not worry, saying, 'What shall we eat?' or 'What shall we drink?' or 'What shall we wear?' For the pagans run after all these things, and your heavenly Father knows that you need them. But seek first his kingdom and his righteousness, and all these things will be given to you as well. Therefore do not worry about tomorrow, for tomorrow will worry about itself. Each day has enough trouble of its own.

(Matthew 6:19-21, 25-34)

Jesus tells his disciples not to be anxious but to trust in a Father's care. He illustrates God's care from nature, and teaches the futility of worry. But to receive a command not to be anxious isn't very easy to handle. It's not easy just to 'switch off' fear or anxiety. So he first gives them the focus to their thinking that will make it possible. He talks of 'storing up treasures in heaven'. He calls us to have a focus on heaven, not this world, in our ambitions and aspirations. Here, 'heaven' speaks to us of God's realm, of his rule. It is the place where God's will is perfectly done. It speaks to us of the invisible things which are in fact more substantial and enduring than the visible things that seem so real and lasting to us.

Invisible things are in fact more substantial and enduring than visible things

In effect, it's almost as if Jesus is teaching that if we get heaven and earth in perspective, his commands to us to be trusting and fearless are really quite easy! Certainly, if we are wrestling with God's call to serve him overseas and

My Rights? My God?

make financial sacrifices, this is a good place for us to spend time, in our thinking and praying.

God's plans for us are that some – not many! – are entrusted with wealth. Whether we are wealthy or not, we can never lay claim to wealth. We have no rights to it. But as his child you do have a right to trust in the Father's care. He has promised us that. And that gives more security than all the gold in Fort Knox.

Do you fear that God may be calling you to something too hard for you? Let's bring the curtain down on this chapter with the words of Jim Elliot, the martyr missionary to the Auca Indians:

'He is no fool who gives what he cannot keep to gain what he cannot lose.'

———

My thoughts

My Rights? My God?

Jenny and Marty's story

Jenny and Marty and their two sons (then aged seven and five) moved to a Central Asian country in 1994. After completing his MBA at Boston University in 1988, Marty had worked in manufacturing and then as the head of finance and administration for the Inter-Varsity Christian Fellowship of Canada. Jenny was a family doctor in a successful and highly satisfying medical practice in Ontario, Canada. Marty takes up the story:

'We both greatly enjoyed our work and felt our gifts and skills were used well. Job satisfaction for both of us was high. We had always intended to go overseas at some point and realised that as our children got older, it was not going to get easier, and that the sense of call was now. We were accepted for service with Interserve - Canada, and now work with IFES as "tent-makers" in Central Asia.

'One of the greatest shocks to us - and one that we had not anticipated - was that job satisfaction simply disappeared. We felt discouraged in our language learning, and chores for daily living took up most of the rest of our time. Then suddenly I had to take over a business that was on the verge of failure. It got difficult for the boys too. After a couple of "easy and fun" months, our elder son experienced a high dose of culture shock and fear. He was in the first grade of a local school which taught in Russian, and he was trying to learn the language and survive.

'Jenny and I had been used to working among skilled and competent professionals and with all kinds of excellent support services. The amazing infrastructure of modern Western life from good roads to dependable lab tests to banking services was where and how we had lived. Canada is consistently rated by the UN as having the world's highest standard of living.

'It was a massive cultural shift. The huge majority of people in the former Soviet states were 50 to 80 years behind in the way they lived, and in their working environments. Often there was no heat, no computers, no basic knowledge of pharmacology or sterilisation, no travellers' cheques or credit cards, and a work ethic that goes with a welfare-military state where no relationship exists between performance and pay.

'We found virtually nothing on which to claim success, and daily failure seemed the rule. We knew in theory that our true identity should be in Christ, but in practice it felt that our identity was in our work, and going down fast. We had a lot to learn.

My Rights? My God?

'Coming to terms with failure and with much lower expectations of what can be done in a day took a long time. It helped to think through what is most important and to focus on that. When so much of Western energy is devoted to money and entertainment, endless education and retirement planning, it takes time to sort out what is really important. Maybe we are beginning to learn.'

Marty Bell is Central Asia Co-ordinator for the International Fellowship of Evangelical Students (IFES).

Chapter 3

Career prospects

Marty and Jenny's situation is a tough one. Some people might think it was a waste of training and abilities which could have been put to better use in their native Canada. They might argue that the skills they have gained should have been ploughed back into the country which paid for their education. The plain sense of that argument seems to hold water, but only in a simple arithmetical kind of framework.

Others will say that as God has given them these gifts, they have the right to use them to best advantage and in a culture which will stretch them. There is no point, they will reason, in taking sophisticated learning to a part of the world which has an undeveloped infrastructure. This too sounds persuasive, but let's note the perspective it is coming from.

This is God's world

How do we respond in either case? Let's start by sketching out some of the biblical framework for how we ought to think of our work in this world. We should note first that there is something of an ambiguity in how the Bible views the world.

On the one hand, we are taught that it is God's world. He made it, he owns it and he rules it. Our sinfulness doesn't change that. It is now a world under judgment, yet still he loves it and cares for it. 'He has compassion on all he has made' says the Psalmist (Psalm 145:9). He sets in place – and deposes – the rulers of the nations (Romans 13:1). As the Dutch theologian Abraham Kuyper once said: 'There is no square foot on the face of the earth of which Jesus Christ may not say, "That is mine!"' And Christians have generally agreed that the commission to develop and care for the world which God gave in the opening chapters of Genesis is still in force. We have made a mess of that task, and still do, but the job remains ours.

Education, industry, medicine, politics, law, environmental protection, whatever – all these play a part in God's ordering of the world. And we can pursue all these as service to God, as outworkings of his 'common grace' to the world. So, if that is where God calls us, there is value and dignity before him in a career in the world. Having this grasp of its being God's world means we can see the whole of our lives as part of that high aspiration to please him in all we do (see 2 Corinthians 5:9).

> There is value and dignity in a career

Of course, because we are a fallen race, we make a mess of things. By our nature as sinful human beings, we spoil the work we do, and we also corrupt our motives in what we do. So what is intended to be the service of God our Creator becomes a means of self-promotion at the expense of others and of God's world. Our godly service soon becomes nothing more worthy than selfish ambition stamped with the logo of the company or the emblem of the college. Careerism rules OK. Instead of being in the service of God, our career and our gifts

My Rights? My God?

become our gods. But we are told to keep ourselves from idols (1 John 5:21).

And that brings us to the other side of the ambiguity.

This is a fallen world

The other way in which the Bible sees 'the world' is not as the wonderful creation of God but as the sphere in which rebellion continues to be played out by creatures against their Creator. This is the 'world' that we are told will hate us because it hated Jesus (John 15:18). This is the 'world' that we are encouraged to see as transient. This is the 'world' we are warned to avoid, not to love (1 John 2:15). This 'world' is the spirit that can seduce us into total absorption in our careers, and make us more concerned to be admired by others than approved by God.

It is not for nothing that John Stott's exposition of the Sermon on the Mount is entitled 'Christian Counter-culture'. Those who are Christ's and have God's Spirit in them belong to a different sphere. We have a different 'citizenship' (Philippians 3:20). While we accept the call to serve in this world we are not of this world. And no matter how much we might earn the appreciation and admiration of 'the world', sooner or later – if we live consistently with our faith – people will find something unusual about us. No matter how fully we play a role in this world, they will see that we march to a different drum.

These two aspects of the world put us in some sort of tension. Christians haven't always managed to keep the balance between affirming the world and denying it. Both find their place in the Bible, but through the years the Church has often gone to one extreme or the other.

Yet to grasp this 'in-between' or 'both-and' position is wonderfully liberating. It is part of the freedom we find in Christ. Those around us, often claiming to be free, are imprisoned in the world's rat race. Christ enables us to be involved in this world while not being 'engrossed' in it. (See the comment on 1 Corinthians 7 in the last chapter.) This gives us a framework for seeing how both going abroad and serving at home can equally find a place in how God uses us.

The potter and the clay

Of course, when we see our work as part of our service to God, certain things follow. He is Lord! The biblical picture that sets this out clearly is that of the potter and the clay. The potter chooses what kind of pot to make with each piece of clay, and the pot isn't entitled to object! We are his clay. He then has the authority to redirect our service into whichever channels he chooses. He knows what is the best use of the gifts he has given us. It is not 'interference' on his part if he re-allocates us to service overseas.

Sometimes that call is to use the same gifts and training that we have been exercising in our home country. For example, he calls some to be 'tent-makers', to take up secular positions in other countries. This may be the best route for reaching places closed to more explicit forms of Christian service. As 'Christian professionals', we might find ourselves playing a role very similar to the one we were doing in our home countries. And alongside the opportunities we have of bringing the message of Christ to our host country, we are able to use our skills to make a contribution to its development, and its people's wellbeing.

On the other hand, God has the prerogative to change our direction more radically, and bring out other gifts in us. He might steer us into spheres where our past training seems quite irrelevant. Sometimes our friends, family or church leaders can find that hard to accept. It can seem a waste, a misuse of resources, a squandering of opportunities. But God is in charge, and his use of his resources is governed by his wisdom and power. Wonderfully, we usually find that more of the lessons learned in our previous occupation carry over into our new sphere than we would ever have imagined.

> Lessons carry over into our new sphere

Do you know how to fail?

Marty Bell could, I know, have written more on the stark contrasts between his and Jenny's present roles and the stimulation and fulfilment they both found back in Canada. There was no sense of success any more. No coming home at the end of the day feeling he had achieved something.

> There was no sense of success any more

I remember talking with a missionary doctor in an outpatients' clinic in a developing country in Africa. He drew my attention to one of the patients and explained her condition. What could be done for her? With the facilities available in his home country – a great deal. With their current facilities – nothing! She would soon be dead. For a professional who is used to being able to save lives by drawing on high-tech up-to-date drugs and equipment, that's hard to accept. It's a blow to one's professionalism.

This sense of failure is not uncommon amongst those who move from high professional standards at home to the conditions of deprivation that are all too common. That can be true of any form of Christian service, of course. We need God to make us less sure of our own resources and more reliant on his. One 'tent-maker' in a tough situation tells how, when talking to potential fellow-workers, he asks them, 'Do you know how to fail?'

It's a Lordship issue

Another potential loss arises for those who come

to re-enter their profession in their home countries. You may find your potential for re-entry has been reduced by a spell overseas. In many professions there used to be a positive attitude to a period of work abroad. It was seen as an attractive addition to one's CV. That is not so common today, at least in the West. Once you have moved out it becomes increasingly difficult to return. So, more and more, when you opt for service abroad you might be burning your professional bridges.

Here the 'rights' question can raise its head again! 'Don't I have the right to exercise my gifts, training and opportunities to the maximum? Why should God call on me to make this sacrifice?'

God is the only one with real rights! It does us no harm to remind ourselves of that. 'You are not your own; you were bought at a price' (1 Corinthians 6:19,20). We shall look at this again in the final chapter. In the self-orientated climate that surrounds us, it can be hard to come to terms with this, but there's no escaping it. And it is wise to settle it in our minds before the testing time comes, so that it takes root in our thinking. As an older missionary remarked to me, 'It's a Lordship issue'.

God is the only one with real rights!

It helps us to remember why it is that God calls some people to walk this road. Like Paul (see Romans 1:14,15), we have an obligation. Paul speaks of his being a 'debtor' to the nations, having an obligation to play his part in bringing the gospel of Christ to those who haven't heard. If we don't go, who will? And then how will they hear? So there's a powerful reason to go, powerful enough to outweigh our sacrifices.

This gives a wonderful value to our role. What greater privilege than to play a part in bringing the light of Christ to people for whom he died? How can we really

My Rights? My God?

compare that with the best that the world can give? Take all your honours and rewards: what will they matter after a few years? And your acceptance by professional peers? Put that alongside the penetrating words of Jesus: 'How can you believe if you accept praise from one another, yet make no effort to obtain the praise that comes from the only God?' (John 5:44).

Let's keep our sacrifices in perspective. They will be real; it would be foolish to pretend otherwise. But Jesus himself promised that we will be generously compensated. 'A hundred times,' he said (Matthew 19:29). The mission field is not full of missionaries bemoaning their lot! Most have already proved the truth of Christ's promise, in one form or another. Christ's service, even when it is costly, is true wealth, not deprivation. Consider the force of Jesus' words in the parable of the rich fool (Luke 12:13-21). The fool is described as 'not rich towards God'.

> Christ's service, even when it is costly, is true wealth, not deprivation

The path the fool has neglected is not really one of poverty but of true riches – of being rich towards God. Rich with the character God creates in his children. Rich with the joy of fellowship with the living God.

Let's see our losses in the light of Paul's consuming ambition:

I consider everything a loss compared to the surpassing greatness of knowing Christ Jesus my Lord, for whose sake I have lost all things. I consider them rubbish, that I may gain Christ and be found in him... I want to know Christ and the power of his resurrection and the fellowship of sharing in his sufferings, becoming like him in his death... Not that I have already obtained all this, or have already been made perfect, but I press on to take hold of that for which Christ Jesus took hold of me. Brothers, I do not consider myself yet to have taken hold of it. But one thing I do: Forgetting what is behind and straining toward what is ahead, I press on toward the goal to win the prize for which God has called me heavenward in Christ Jesus.

(Philippians 3:8-14)

Recommended reading

Jonathan Lewis (ed), *Working Your Way to the Nations: A Guide to Effective Tentmaking* (William Carey Library)
Michael Griffiths, *Tinker, Tailor, Missionary* (IVP)
Dick Dowsett, *God, that's not fair!* (OMF/STL)

My Rights? My God?

My thoughts

Kevin and Liz Wren's story: Living on the 'beach'

Living on the beach may sound romantic, but perhaps we should rephrase that to living beside the rubbish tip, as that's the nearest thing we could really compare it to. It wasn't luxury, but we'd never been so happy and excited as we felt then.

Our neighbours were down to earth, fun-loving people, despite their extreme poverty. They had time on their hands, so they always wanted to chat with us. This made us feel at home and was great for our language practice. They were also generous, always giving us fish that they'd caught. And they took Kevin fishing too.

As our homes were so close, we were with them from morning till night. Our house was newly-built and made of concrete, with two rooms upstairs and one downstairs, plus a shower/toilet. The fishermen's bamboo huts had neither shower nor toilet. They washed under the water pump outside our kitchen window, and used the beach and the sea as a toilet. In the mornings we heard them going out to fish, any time from 3am onwards.

Life could be hard and stressful, and we tired easily and needed to keep our spiritual lives in good shape. But we loved the wonderful chance to get into the local language, and the friendly atmosphere in which to witness. The first time that I (Liz) saw my nearest neighbour, I was frightened of her. She was well-built, and her decibel level would have made anyone jump. A couple of days later I was woken in the night by her youngest child crying. I was frightened to go and see what was wrong, but felt I had to. The little boy was sick, so I gave her some Calpol for him. At 4.30am I heard excited voices outside telling the story of how the 'foreign' woman had come to help.

After this, we became friends. They started to visit us often, to chat, cook, eat, and look at our photographs. The local children started to come, too, to play with Jonathan and Matthew and with their toys.

We laughed a lot. We had to. I (Kevin) remember talking to one of the fishermen's wives when her baby wet his underpants. (They didn't use nappies.) She just took them off and hung them on the fence to dry. A bit later in the conversation the baby's nose was running. So she got the underpants off the fence and wiped his nose on them!

We wrote to our prayer partners and asked them to give thanks with us for our home and our new friends. And we urged them to pray that God would move by his Spirit so the fishermen in Lemery [Philippines] would choose to follow him, just as Peter and Andrew had in Galilee.

Kevin and Liz Wren are British workers with OMF International.

My Rights? My God?

Chapter 4

Entering another's world

I t's a funny business, this process of entering another culture. Many of us have at least some acquaintance with it, but for most of us that's where it stops. We watch television documentaries. We may reach the level of the tourist. But we don't know what it's like to live there.

We tend to underestimate the differences between cultures. We see them simply in terms of skin colour or language, with perhaps a passing nod to differences of customs. And we often react with prejudice. Those who study ethnic prejudice tell us that when we perceive a difference – any difference – between ourselves and someone else, we attach a value to it, and it is usually a negative one. Even differences of regional accents within our own country can trigger prejudice! So we view those who grew up in a different state or a different county as superior or inferior without realising it. National pride and racism find their roots in that kind of thinking.

> When we perceive a difference, we attach a value to it

And all this is happening before we've finished watching the television documentary on another country, or finished surfing the web for a cheap flight somewhere.

Next stage, the tourist! It's holiday time, and the name of the game is novelty and fascination. New sights, sounds, smells. New scenery, unfamiliar customs, an unknown language. Things to talk about in the refectory or the office when we get home. And even if the hotel is noisy and you get a touch of gastro trouble, it won't last long. You'll be home next week. Home, where they use proper money and speak a proper language and you know where to buy toothpaste and what the shop assistant will call it! The key word for the tourist is 'temporary'. You aren't there long enough to know what it means to live there.

It's the long stay that is the crunch. Now it's not just how to find the campsite telephone or the hotel dining room. You need more language skills than asking the way to the post office, phrase-book style. You may not be within ready reach of those zillions of bank machines the banks tell you about in their glossy literature. You could have to spend three hours in a queue in the bank, as the locals do. We need a whole range of information and skills when we have to live, and to fend for ourselves, in a foreign culture.

When the local people and their ways are no longer novelties, they may no longer seem so interesting. (And perhaps you are no longer a novelty to them!) In fact, many things about them begin to be irritating and even threatening. The local culture can begin to look 'inferior' to your own. National pride, that you thought you would never be guilty of, flares up inside you.

If you manage to find a group of fellow expatriates, their company can be like an oasis in the desert. It can be like a magnet, and you can find yourself drawn to it for a sense of safety and security. You are in culture shock. And you may be starting to understand how complex 'culture' is.

Retreating like that may be OK if we don't need to relate to the local people in any meaningful way. But if

My Rights? My God?

they are really the whole reason why we're there, we need to find a better solution.

Culture is more complex than you think

Why is this process of entering another culture such a battle? First, because culture is so much more complicated than we realise, and also because our own culture is 'transparent' to us. We are like a goldfish in a bowl. He can look through the glass and see the outside world, but he can't see the water that is his own world. Our culture is drip-fed into us from our earliest months, and we live it unconsciously. We don't think of ourselves as *practising* our culture: we simply are what we *are*! And we unconsciously assume that all humans function as we do.

> Culture is much more complicated than we realise

What is culture? One definition goes like this: *Culture is all learned behaviour which is socially acquired, that is, the material and nonmaterial traits which are passed on from one generation to another.* Thus the ability to eat is instinctive, not learned, and is not part of culture. But different ways of eating – knife and fork, chopsticks, fingers – are learned: they are part of 'culture'. The ability to sing is not 'culture', but using twelve tones to the octave, or five, is socially acquired, and is 'culture'.

Another example. We all use our hands to pass things to someone else, or to receive things from them. That is what hands are designed for, and isn't culture. But some people-groups teach their children, from their earliest years, that it is proper to use only the right hand for this, never the left. They use the left hand only for personal hygiene, and it is 'unclean' for other uses. Their children grow up instinctively and quite unconsciously using their right hands, not left, for that. To be forced to use the left hand would be awkward, offensive, embarrassing! That is part of their culture.

The same principles arise in all sorts of behaviour patterns. How we ask questions, how groups come to collective decisions, how the genders and the generations treat each other, and so on. And just as we may be unconscious of our own cultural distinctive, many in our host country will be unconscious of theirs. We may find we relate to them with minimal trouble, even without our or their being very conscious of the cultural gulf – until the moment we say or do something that is completely natural to us, but that is unnatural, and perhaps offensive, to them.

I remember watching a group of young people in an African town. There were perhaps eight of them, including two Westerners. At first, they were chatting freely and happily among themselves, but then I noticed that the African members of the group had gone silent. The Westerners carried on, oblivious to the change. Clearly they had said something, in all ignorance, that cut across the African cultural norms. (As I recall, the difference was in the area of how generations relate to one another.) I sensed the Africans were mystified, rather than offended, by the Westerners' different underlying assumptions.

I sensed the Africans were mystified, rather than offended

Of course, the offence can be the other way round. A young missionary couple are working in a village in the Philippines. They live in a house that opens straight onto the street. Some of their windows, likewise, open onto the street. They describe how difficult they found it when the villagers, in a way quite natural to them, would spend perhaps half an hour standing outside the windows, peering in! In the West we guard our privacy quite jealously. We close our front doors and draw our

In the West we guard our privacy jealously

My Rights? My God?

In the West we guard our privacy jealously...
but this can be a price we are called to pay.

curtains when it gets dark. We're home. We can choose whether to answer the doorbell, or the phone. We can choose whether to download email or have an evening without any intrusion whatsoever: human, voice or electronic. We are in charge. But this young couple cannot do that. They have chosen to forgo what Westerners consider their inalienable right. It can be hard not to resent people behaving in ways that intrude on us, or cause us inconvenience, and even offence. But that may be a price we are called to pay.

Getting to the point where we can live effectively in another culture, and have relationships beyond the superficial, takes time and effort. It's not easy, and it's not always pleasant or comfortable. I was struck by the way Kevin and Liz Wren had handled this in their first term in the Philippines, when they were just out of language school. They believed the Lord wanted them to live in a particular town, but there wasn't anywhere available to rent. So they settled for a house among the fishermen on the beach. It was no picnic, as you'll have seen from their story. But the Wrens are no ordinary couple. Kevin left school at seventeen and became an itinerant evangelist. He learned the art of fire-eating, which could often draw a crowd! Liz trained as a nurse. After they had been married a short time, both sensed God's call on their lives, and they started to explore the possibility of working in Asia. It would be a wrench to leave families and friends behind, and Liz felt that keenly. But as they talked and prayed about it they found themselves echoing the apostle Paul's words: 'the love of Christ leaves us no choice' (2 Corinthians 5:14). They have since moved elsewhere in East Asia, to an area where their neighbours are all Muslims. And again they're learning another new culture, building friendships, building trust, to serve that community.

He learned the art of fire-eating, which could draw a crowd!

My Rights? My God?

Do I *need* to change?

This is a good question. Learning to live in our host culture won't be easy. At times it will feel like a denial of our very identity. Why should I put up with that inconvenience? Haven't I the right just to be myself? If that's how God has shaped me, can't I stay that way?

The issue is underlined when we see how far some people go in maintaining an environment that reflects their home culture. Their homes, even their cars, are little enclaves of America or Europe.

> Their homes are little enclaves of America or Europe

Of course, there is a limit to the extent we can or need to 'become like them'. No matter how long you live in your host culture, and no matter what efforts you make to conform to it, you can never become fully one of them. It's just not possible. Even where you come to behave as they do, it will often be behaviour that you have consciously learned and may still exercise consciously. They have acquired it unconsciously and exercise it unconsciously, as we all do in our own culture. We may well adopt some parts of their behaviour unconsciously, but other things – even when we get it almost right – will always be done consciously. So it is futile to hope to be able to become completely like them.

Neither would they expect us to become completely like them. We may reach a stage when we are so comfortable in our host culture that we feel quite inconspicuous. Yet our friends from the host culture will always be aware of our foreignness, and they accept that as part of us. They take it for granted; it is not resented. In fact, attempts to go too far can come across as strained, artificial, even patronising. They welcome the efforts we

> Our friends will always be aware of our foreignness, and accept that as part of us

make to show respect to their culture and be able to relate well to them. They don't expect us to become one of them.

Well then, do you *have* to change? If you have any thoughts of serving the people in your host country, then surely the answer has to be yes!

Look again at the person who strives to make every part of his environment as much like 'being back home' as he can. Make no mistake, his national friends will notice it. What signal does it give to them? It tells them that he would rather be home than in their country. Beyond that, it tells them that their Western friend is not only attached to his own culture (that would be accepted) but more, that he dislikes – even despises – theirs. They suspect that he thinks of his own culture as the truly Christian culture, superior in all respects to their own.

That view of our cultures is simply false! No culture deserves to be set up as *the* Christian culture: no culture ever has. Even if we can't see the blemishes in our own cultures, or the areas where our friends' culture is better, we may be sure they will. If, deep down, we believe our culture is superior to theirs, and betray that in our attitudes, we will certainly close their ears to what we might hope to tell them.

> No culture deserves to be set up as *the* Christian culture: no culture ever has

Think of some of the cultural features where there are differences between 'us' and 'them'. Take, for example, the ways of speaking that are seen as 'good manners'. Suppose that, after some time in our host country, we are still making the same mistakes we made in our early days, so that our friends wince as much at our apparent bad manners now as they did then. We'll simply appear rude to them. They will certainly find it impossible to believe that we love them. At best, their ears are likely to be closed to our message. At worst, they will avoid us or even

My Rights? My God?

treat us with hostility. Frankly, we will deserve it! If we are there to serve the King, the cost will include the pain and inconvenience of entering the world of our hosts.

What can we learn from Paul?

We can expect to find some light on this from the apostle Paul, the great missionary pioneer. Take, for example, the explanation he gives to the church in Corinth of some of his principles (1 Corinthians chapter 9). Seven times in this chapter he uses the word 'right' or 'rights', and he claims certain rights. Then, in passionate language he sets out what matters more than these rights. His point in claiming them is to show that he is willing to give them up. In verse 19 he spells out the main principle:

> Though I am free and belong to no man, I make myself a slave to everyone, to win as many as possible.

Then he applies this to a range of issues – including cultural differences – that he faced in his ministry:

> To the Jews I became like a Jew, to win the Jews. To those under the law I became like one under the law (though I myself am not under the law), so as to win those under the law. To those not having the law I became like one not having the law (though I am not free from God's law but am under Christ's law), so as to win those not having the law. To the weak I became weak, to win the weak.
> (vv 20-22)

His principle was to adapt, where possible, to the cultures of those he aimed to reach. So in a final summarising statement he tells us:

> I have become all things to all men so that by all possible means I might save some. I do all this for the sake of the gospel, that I may share in its blessings. (vv 22,23)

For Paul, what was best for the gospel overshadowed his 'rights'.

> For Paul, what was best for the gospel overshadowed his 'rights'

A wise remark of John Calvin's on a closely related theme illustrates Paul's mind. Dealing with Christian liberty, Calvin remarks that Christian liberty is not lost, even if it is never exercised.[1] Our aggressive and self-assertive world would tell us that the essence of freedoms is to exercise them, and the

> Christian liberty is not lost, even if it is never exercised

essence of rights is to demand them. No, says Calvin, reflecting the spirit shown here by Paul. If, for the sake of others, I choose not to exercise my freedom, I am in no way less free. So Paul writes, 'Though I am free and belong to no man, I make myself a slave to everyone, to win as many as possible'. 'Though I *am* free', note, not 'Though I *was* free'. The truly free man or woman is free to exercise a right or not to exercise it! Either way, they remain free, if they choose in this spirit of service to others.

Let's turn to a higher example – that of the Lord Jesus Christ himself. We need to be careful about drawing parallels between Christ's experiences and ours: nothing that we might ever be called on to endure can compare with his humiliation in becoming a man and dying for us. But we are encouraged in Scripture to look at him as an example for us in some things. Surely this is one.

In Philippians chapter 2, Paul tells his readers to imitate Christ (see verse 5). In what way? In his willingness not to hold on to his 'right' to enjoy his status of equality with God. In this immeasurably costly identification with us, which Paul spells out for us step by breath-taking step, Christ goes down, not only to become man but to die. Not only to die but to die a criminal's humiliating death (vv 6-8).

My Rights? My God?

He was called to do more than we could ever be called to. In Paul's terse phrase, 'he made himself nothing'.

Some other words of Paul's come to mind – good words to muse on as we close this chapter. Once more, Paul is using Christ as an example for us to follow:

> You know the grace of our Lord Jesus Christ, that though he was rich, yet for your sakes he became poor, so that you through his poverty might become rich.
>
> (2 Corinthians 8:9)

We have the gospel. We are rich. In a pale reflection of the Lord's ministry to us, will we 'become poor' to take this gospel to others?

Recommended reading

Paul Hiebert, *Anthropological Insights for Missionaries* (Baker Book House).

Notes

1. John Calvin, *Institutes of the Christian Religion*, Book III, Chapter 19.

———

My thoughts

My Rights? My God?

Stephen and Jill's story

(The names below are fictitious, and the story, while not an exact record of any situation, is a true reflection of many.)

Stephen and Jill met at Bible College, where both were preparing for long-term cross-cultural service.

Their first year abroad was marked by good progress with language and culture acquisition, and promising ministry in the urban environment. People remarked on Stephen's excellent relationships with the nationals. At the end of that year they were allocated to a rural Bible College teaching post. Some doubted the wisdom of this allocation, as there had been a history of misunderstandings between the mission and church leaders in that community. But they threw themselves into the work with great zeal and early days were trouble-free.

Very soon, Stephen was asked to take on a more senior role in the college, which he did. This was not without its strains, however, and it soon put him under pressure. Then the difficulties began.

Embarking on this ministry brought him face to face with local realities. Stephen is a gifted and able man, and like many such people, he sets high standards for himself - and for others! Some students couldn't match them, and they resented his position. Some decisions had been taken by national administrative staff which he felt further undermined the drive for good academic standards, and he was not happy about this. He felt that problems needed to be addressed, and he set about doing so. The tensions increased, and included student protests.

Missionary colleagues were divided, some supporting him in his position, others feeling he was impatient and not sufficiently respecting of the church leadership. This probably reflected the range of personalities and cultures within the mission team as much as it did the issues!

National leaders, too, were divided, some opposing him while others continued to respect and value him.

The situation reached stalemate, and attempts at reconciliation proved fruitless. As in many such situations, there were probably rights and wrongs on both sides, and the conflict might well have been as much due to 'style' as to 'substance'. In the end, Stephen and Jill, hurt and confused, were re-allocated elsewhere. Time will tell what lessons can be learned from the whole painful episode.

My Rights? My God?

Chapter 5

Expectations in our ministry

Who owns the vineyard?

We live in an age when Christians are in danger of becoming pre-occupied with finding 'fulfilment'. Is that to be found in exercising our gifts to the full? Even if it is, do we have a right to it? Should it be our goal? The 'me generation' seems to think so.

There is, of course, a grain of truth here. The gifts God gives us are entrusted to us to use well. That, after all, is why we might be thinking of going abroad. We believe we have a message to bring, a contribution to make.

We enter our host country with a set of expectations about our potential usefulness. After all, it's surely not for nothing that God has called us to serve him there. And our gifts and experience at home have equipped us with something to bring to those we will live among. That's a sound way of thinking. In fact we should probably not be considering service overseas unless we have already shown in our home country that God has given us the gifts for it.

Beyond doubt, we work most effectively in activities that fit the gifts God has given us. And it can be a very rewarding experience. But God also calls us to think first of being useful to him and to others, and only second of our own fulfilment. It's rather like happiness in the Christian life. Have you noticed how those who make the pursuit of happiness their supreme goal become the most miserable people? Nothing can compare with the happiness that God gives to those who, like Paul, 'make it our goal to please him' (2 Corinthians 5:9).

> Have you noticed how those who make the pursuit of happiness their supreme goal become the most miserable people?

I can still hear the passionate voice of a senior missionary as he addressed a leaders' conference. He was speaking on Jesus' parable of the tenants in Mark 12:1-12. Do you recall how the owner of the vineyard finally sent his son to collect his payment? The tenants then said to one another, 'This is the heir. Come, let's kill him, and the inheritance will be ours'. The speaker pressed home this question: 'Who owns the vineyard?' We all know the answer. The question is, do we act as if we do? Do we acknowledge his rights? Or do we think of our gifts and ministry as if we were the owners rather than the trustees? This is not a lesson we learn once and for all in Bible college, or in our first term of service. It is something we need to come to terms with over and over again, as servants of Christ. Something we need to take ourselves in hand about. Something we need to ask others to pray for, for us. Our commitment is to Christ, and not to our own fulfilment. This commitment will be tested time and again as we serve abroad.

Learning a different drumbeat

Some cultures are as pressured and as 'driven' as our own. Others have lifestyles which travel at a very

My Rights? My God?

different pace. We may think them inefficient, and in many ways they are. But let us not be quite so quick to judge. We should not overlook the weaknesses of our own backgrounds. Those from slower cultures will perceive things we miss. They may think us deficient, unable to measure our pace and get more out of life's various experiences.

To the Westerner, time can be all-important. It is measurable – in hours, minutes, seconds. It can be saved or wasted. Perhaps those in our host country think more about its *value* than its *length*: what you *do* with it is what matters. They may rate occasion and relationships more highly, and may be the better for that. We will find ourselves being enriched, and gaining fresh insights, if we adapt our pace a little to their drumbeat. There are things we can learn here.

I recall some shrewd observations from three women missionaries who crossed the Gobi Desert five times by horse and cart. They were a remarkable trio, by any standards. Addressing a crowd in London just before returning to the nomads and traders of the Silk Road for their final term of service, one of them said this:

> At home, all is for speed, but the ancient roads, with their three miles per hour, are better suited for the great business of preaching the gospel. Christ joined himself to two discouraged disciples on the road, and the talk was about great things. The great question of the road is 'Where have you come from and where are you going?' Think what you lose by speed. You can't talk of these great and everlasting subjects when speed is the passion.[1]

All this can mean that the process of gaining acceptance in another culture is slower too. One frustration can be the delay in finding opportunities for ministry. We set off to our new sphere filled with energy and zeal, eager to get stuck in. But instead of doors opening, they remain stubbornly closed. Instead of our gifts and experience being recognised, we are left on the sidelines.

We are tempted to think we would have been more useful if we had stayed at home. We might have had a fulfilling role pastoring a church or leading a youth ministry, working among people we knew and understood. We may find ourselves resentful, feeling that the church leaders in our host country must lack discernment, or they would recognise straight away what we can do for them. We can even find ourselves despising them. Our emotions can run high. Is this the price we have to pay? Is that reasonable? Did we come to this country just to vegetate? What's going on?

Did we come to this country just to vegetate?

Even at home it takes time to become accepted and recognised in a new situation. Perhaps we are experiencing nothing more than that. This feature of change of role is common to every move in life. But if we haven't experienced it before, it can come as a shock, and if we are struggling with a new language at the same time, it can be extremely difficult to handle. It can take us by surprise and be very frustrating. It is one of the real tests of our willingness to let God be God in our lives, and let him control the way he uses our gifts.

Added to this, the cultures we find in many developing countries have very different attitudes to youth and age from those in our home countries. Many nations have a greater respect for age and experience, and may be less inclined to make way for younger people. We need to respect their cultural distinctives and be patient with the process. In the process, we will come to appreciate our host culture more and learn valuable lessons.

Many nations may be less inclined to make way for younger people

We need to be aware of how we come across. Perhaps without realising it, we may seem patronising. We may even be perceived as showing national pride. It is much harder for us to avoid this than we sometimes realise. National pride is a subtle and insidious thing. It is so easy for us to behave in ways that convey a message of superiority without meaning to. No surprise, then, if people don't rush to make much of us, or to give us positions of prominence!

Whatever the factors at play, if we are to be truly useful to those we serve, we need to learn lessons of patience and humility. Is it our 'right' to have our gifts and ministry recognised? Well, no, it isn't. And in the end, God's pace in this process is best and will lead to greater effectiveness.

> If we are to be truly useful, we need to learn lessons of patience and humility

George Whitefield, one of the great preachers in the 18th-century spiritual awakening in the UK and the USA, was an unwearying activist. Often, when he had preached himself into the ground and was on the point of collapse, he would find himself fired up by a fresh opportunity, with all his energies restored! In his ministry he crossed the Atlantic thirteen times, but not in a jumbo jet at 500 mph, of course. His travel was in a sailing ship, on a journey that took weeks, not hours.

The activist in him seized the opportunity of preaching to everyone on board! But when he had done all that he could of that, he had only reading and writing left to spend the days on. Initially, he chafed at this 'loss' of time. But at one point he records in his journal, 'I have learned that the reaper is not wasting his time when he is whetting his scythe.' He learned to see the benefit of God's 'sharpening' and to submit to it with a more patient spirit.

We could do worse than learn from George

Whitefield, when our 'journey' to ministry opportunities seems slow. Sharpen the scythe!

Why don't they do things my way?

We all start off thinking that the way we handle things is better than the way other cultures do. Perhaps we even believe there is no other way of doing things! We soon realise otherwise. Experience brings home to us that other cultures solve some common human problems very differently. Wisdom may teach us that in some cases their answers are better than ours. And sometimes, of course, they simply get it wrong – just as we all do.

These differences can be instructive; they can also be frustrating. We can find frustration in watching the way they make decisions or resolve conflict (including the way they handle church discipline). Typically, people in many two-thirds-world cultures are less confrontational than Westerners, and this comes out clearly in areas of conflict. Sometimes it will seem to a Western observer that the issue is simply being avoided. When a matter is taken forward, progress can seem intolerably slow.

Our customs in these areas are sometimes better, sometimes worse – or sometimes just different! When we first encounter these differences we would be wise to suspend our judgment at first, and watch and listen. Stephen and Jill's story may be an example. Perhaps Stephen should have been slower to evaluate how his host culture was functioning. Our first mistake is often not one of judgment, but of understanding wrongly. We jump to make value judgments on how an unfamiliar culture 'works' before we've truly understood what's going on. Let's work hard at being slow to come to conclusions.

Stephen's experience probably also illustrates another truth. People from different Western cultures differ

My Rights? My God?

*Delete as appropriate.

from each other! So life can be further complicated by working in a multinational team of missionaries. New missionaries are very aware of the obviously unfamiliar features of their host culture, and are not surprised by them. What they are less prepared for are the differences between Canadian and Australian, British and American and so on.

> Life can be further complicated by working in a multinational team

The struggle comes when we think we know what should be done but can do nothing about it. It may be inappropriate for us, as guests, to appear to criticise our hosts. If we do offer suggestions, they may be ignored or resented. It can be even more difficult when we find that we have to follow lines we disagree with. If the issue is one of principle, then the right course of action for us may be straightforward, if costly. More often, however, the issue is not as clear cut.

A common example is the area of legalism. We may be astonished to find that a style of dress which is completely acceptable in our home country is frowned on in the national churches. It may be as basic as wearing sandals instead of shoes, or an open-necked shirt instead of a collar and tie. In these circumstances, do you have the freedom to follow your own preferences, or do you conform?

If the other person's position is just mildly 'narrow' (like style of dress), we may decide the wiser course is simply to accept it. Paul's encouragement to us to submit to one another would apply (Ephesians 5:21). But the decision becomes more difficult if we feel it undermines the gospel (as Paul concluded Peter's behaviour in Antioch did: see Galatians chapter 2). Toeing the line can be the right and gracious way forward, but compromising the gospel would not be. What do we do when one person sees something as an issue of conscience while the other thinks it is comparatively unimportant? Paul's principle of 'the weaker brother' then applies (see 1 Corinthians 8:1-13; 10:23-33). Let each hold to his own view, Paul would teach us, but the one who is 'free' needs to be careful not in any way to put pressure on the other person to do something he regards as wrong. In all of this, the principle seems to be love, and concern for another, without becoming tyrannised by anyone's opinions. Great principles, but not easy to put into practice!

> Toeing the line can be the right and gracious way forward, but compromising the gospel would not be

Matters can also be aggravated by differing attitudes to authority. Expressing a different opinion may be quite acceptable at home. Christians in our host country, however, might see it as disloyal or insubordinate. This same issue of authority can arise in relationships with senior missionary colleagues, especially those in authority over you. You may think they have attitudes to authority that disappeared ten or twenty years ago in your home country. You may feel they have conformed too much to the national churches' views, and have failed to promote biblical teaching on freedom. But we would probably be wise to recognise that our own cultures have moved very far from the biblical standards for accepting authority, and are not necessarily a good guide.

> Our own cultures have moved very far from the biblical standards for accepting authority

How do we react in these situations? What 'rights' can we exercise? Be sure of this: we will meet situations where we find ourselves perplexed. In fact situations like these may be among the most baffling we will ever encounter. Whatever the issue, in most cases the right course will be to say less than we think, and to accept authority more readily than we would like to, or are used to. Can we do that, for the sake of Christ?

Has God changed his mind?

We have thought about opportunities that are slow in coming, and the cost of waiting for them. We have looked at unwelcome constraints on our ministry, and the cost of submission. Perhaps there's another even more demanding scenario.

I recall a missionary couple sitting in my office. Through traumatic circumstances, and through no fault of their own, they had had to leave their work in Africa and return home. In anguish the man cried out, 'Why, Lord, did you give us the vision and not allow us to fulfil it?' It seemed so pointless, all the years of preparation, the years of acquiring the language and culture – for nothing. I felt with them, and I could hear the question going round and round their heads. 'If we have made sacrifices and faced costs for this, should we not be allowed to have a decent stab at it?'

Fortunately, as elsewhere in this book, we might here be looking at something that is not common. But it does happen to some, and we can prepare ourselves for it. We need to lay down in our hearts and minds a foundation of trust in a God who does all things well. A God who is our heavenly Father. A God whose every action in the lives of his children is marked by his wisdom and love. A God whose wise and loving treatment of his children can be very mystifying at the time, but – as history shows – is vindicated by events. (See for example the 'Lessons from China' on the following page.)

In England in the 18th century, the great preacher John Wesley, the founder of Methodism, came across some words written a hundred years earlier to focus people's thoughts on 'making a covenant with God'. Wesley

My Rights? My God?

Lessons from China

In 1949 the Communists came to power in China, and over a fifth of the world's population suddenly came under Communist rule. In the hundred years up to then, it had been possible, though often dangerous, to travel in the country, and to preach Christ. Now that freedom had disappeared.

Over the next two years all missionaries were withdrawn. It was the only option. Chinese Christians associating with foreigners soon came under particular scrutiny from the government. What a painful departure it was. Missionaries sensed that their Christian friends, whom they had nurtured and mentored, would suffer greatly. As they sailed home to Europe, North America, Australia, they could hardly believe what God had allowed to happen. How would the Church survive?

Chairman Mao would have loved to stamp the Church out, but he did not have that power. Through the years that followed it was sometimes hard to find out what was happening, not least during the dark days of the Cultural Revolution. But Christians round the world prayed, and God heard their prayers. Through all its suffering, the Chinese Church not only survived, but it grew. Today it is the largest evangelical community in the world.

One of the missions working in China was the China Inland Mission. In

1952 its leaders met to decide what to do. Was the work founded by Hudson Taylor now complete in God's eyes? No, they sensed, it wasn't. This was when the mission re-formed, becoming what is now OMF International, and those missionaries who had left China sailed for Japan, Thailand, the Philippines and other East Asian countries. They worked first among the Chinese communities, and then more widely with the Japanese, the Thai, the Filipinos... The Church in some of these places is now established under national leadership; in others it is still small and struggling.

Who owns the vineyard? God owns the vineyard. The remarkable account of the suffering and glory of the Chinese Church is rich in lessons on this. God is sovereign, and in his providence he places his workers where he chooses.

took up the words and instituted in the Methodist churches an annual 'Covenant service' at the start of each year. Many Methodist churches around the world still use this. Perhaps its words will help us lay that foundation in our own thoughts. I leave them in their slightly older language; the first paragraph is instruction, the second a response in prayer.

> Christ has many services to be done; some are easy, others are difficult; some bring honour, others bring reproach; some are suitable to our natural inclinations and temporal interests, others are contrary to both. In some we may please Christ and please ourselves, in others we cannot please Christ except by denying ourselves. Yet the power

My Rights? My God?

to do all these things is assuredly given us in Christ, who strengthens us.

I am no longer my own, but thine. Put me to what thou wilt; rank me with whom thou wilt; put me to doing, put me to suffering; let me be employed for thee or laid aside for thee, exalted for thee or brought low for thee; let me be full, let me be empty; let me have all things, let me have nothing; I freely and heartily yield all things to thy pleasure and disposal.'

Don't rush on. Take some time to reflect on these words. The prayer is a very searching one. If this is to be our covenant with God, let us make it that. And perhaps look over the prayer as Wesley urged the Methodists to do, regularly.

Do we *believe* God owns the vineyard?

When Lloyd (see chapter 2), the young Australian, first thought about going abroad with Operation Mobilisation, his friends protested. They said he was already far too useful in Christian work in Australia. It would be a waste of his gifts to pass by the opportunities (summer camps, for example) in which God was already using him.

Lloyd is not alone in that experience. The people God calls abroad are certain to be active in his service wherever they are. They are the people who will be missed!

Yes, there are disadvantages in moving into another culture: the loss of time while we learn another language, the painful process of adapting, the years spent in learning lessons and making mistakes. But let us remind ourselves of the question with which this chapter opened. Who owns the vineyard?

And let us always have in our thinking that gospel plea of Paul in Romans 10:14,15: 'How, then, can they call on the one they have not believed in? And how can they believe in the one of whom they have not heard? And how can they hear without someone preaching to them? And how can they preach unless they are sent?' Someone must go. If everyone, through the centuries, had listened to the reasons for not going, the Church would still be confined to the countries around the Eastern Mediterranean!

> If everyone, through the centuries, had listened to reasons for not going, the Church would still be confined to the Middle East

God has done many wonderful things through the lives of dedicated men and women whom he buried in what seem to us to be unpromising situations. These people took seriously Jesus' teaching that when a grain of wheat 'dies' it bears fruit (John 12:24). Jesus goes on to say, 'The man who loves his life will lose it, while the man who hates his life in this world will keep it for eternal life.' There are men and women who have believed that divine paradox, and their lives have proved it true.

Recommended reading

Ajith Fernando, *An Authentic Servant* (OMF booklet)
D. E. Hoste, *36 Steps to Christian Leadership* (OMF booklet)
Tony Lambert, *China's Christian Millions* (OMF/Monarch)

Notes

1. Mildred Cable, and Francesca and Eva French, known as 'The Trio' were missionaries with the China Inland Mission. Mildred Cable was speaking here.

My Rights? My God?

My thoughts

Janet Brown's story

In 1993 I read *Joy Unspeakable* by Dr Martyn Lloyd Jones. It left me with questions: 'Is there more to following Jesus than I know?' 'Where is the joy he speaks about, in my life?' 'Am I missing out on something?' Not long after this I heard rumours of the 'Toronto Blessing'. For many it seemed to bring renewal and refreshing. A friend who had been dogged with depression for years seemed to be healed overnight. Was this the 'something more' I was seeking? Was this blessing for me?

Now as I write, I finally feel like I have made a tiny step forward in knowing God's blessing. There have been some tough moments… Being airlifted out of war-torn Monrovia by US marines in 1996. We lost everything – friends, home, ministry, possessions and even a sense of vision for what God wanted to do. Being attacked in our home in Côte d'Ivoire soon after arriving to minister to Liberian refugees. Armed men threatening my children's lives and my husband's life. A neighbour being killed, a guard critically wounded. Having anything of 'value' taken. And then the utter shame of being stripped and raped. Where was God? Where was the blessing?

In his book, *When Heaven is Silent*, Ronald Dunn talks of 'strange ministers', that is blessings which are so well disguised that they look like curses. Jacob, struggling with God, is wounded but comes away with a blessing. He had had the 'mountain top' experience of God at Bethel as he slept. He had seen angels descending and ascending on the ladder from heaven, and God had given him some great promises. But it was only in the struggle with God that he was actually changed from 'deceiver and cheat' to 'Israel' (the one who struggles with God). That didn't sound much of a blessing, but it was to change his life forever.

Philippians 3:10 talks of the blessing I want. Paul writes: 'I want to know Christ and the *power* of his resurrection'. Yes, that's the blessing I want! But he doesn't stop there. He goes on to talk of wanting 'the fellowship of sharing in his sufferings' even 'becoming like him in his death' so that he might attain to the resurrection. Do I really want *this* blessing?

I said I had made a *tiny* step since 1993, and it is just a tiny step. I am beginning to see that God wants to change me and bless me. I know that I want to be changed and blessed. But we are not always in agreement about the process; it *is* a struggle!

I want to know Christ and the power of his resurrection. He wants me to understand the fellowship of sharing in his sufferings. The two go together! And it is in seeing the two as working together, not in conflict, that there is a blessing.

My Rights? My God?

Yes, I'd rather have an 'experience', to have God change me painlessly and perfectly, perhaps in a conference or a meeting sometime, somewhere. It can happen to people that way. For me it hasn't (yet), but I can still know God's blessing *in* the struggle.

Father, may we know Christ and the power of his resurrection in our ministry and in our lives. May we willingly share in his sufferings and count our lives no more important than his. I ask this that not only we, but many of every tribe, tongue and nation, will somehow attain to the resurrection from the dead. Amen!

David and Janet Brown served with SIM in Ethiopia, Liberia and Côte d'Ivoire for twelve years, and are now based in the SIM-UK office.

Ruth Clark's story

It was 23 July 1996 and we had been in Ethiopia for six years. I was leaving for a three-day trip as part of my counselling ministry. With my daughter home from boarding school, it was a trip I would have preferred not to make, but because of the special needs in this case I agreed to go. I set out with a pastor, his two young sons, and two Ethiopian friends.

Our journey was to the town of Jimma, eight hours south of Addis Ababa, where we lived. Two hours from Jimma our Land Cruiser was hit head-on by a truck carrying seven tons of coffee beans. The nine-year-old travelling in the middle of the front seat, so with no safety belt, felt a hand against his chest pushing him back against the seat. The next thing he remembered was seeing me fly over him from the middle of the back seat.

They found me unconscious, between the front and back seats. I had seven broken ribs, my left shoulder blade was broken, and I had a head injury. My back was broken just between my shoulder blades, and my spinal cord damaged. Two of the others had broken arms, but the rest were not seriously hurt.

The mission's medical team reached us four hours later, with pain relief medication and other supplies. I had to spend the night in the wrecked car before a helicopter could fly in the next morning, through a break in the clouds, and fly me out to Addis. Late that afternoon I was flown to Nairobi, Kenya, where specialist care is better. It took twenty-eight hours before I arrived at the hospital. Four weeks later, after a long, traumatic flight, I was in Charlotte, USA.

In spite of all the fine medical care that followed, I will be paralysed from my chest down for the rest of my life unless God does a miracle. Our ministry in Ethiopia has ended. I am a paraplegic.

On my first Sunday out of hospital, we were celebrating communion. The pastor explained that the bread represented Jesus' body broken for us, and suddenly a thought hit me and overwhelmed me.

It was as if the Lord were saying, 'Ruth, are you willing for your body to be broken for me?' The fact is…it *is* broken. The question was, 'Are you *willing*?'

Was I *willing*? There it was, right in front of me. I had a choice. That choice was not only for the future, but for every minute of every day and every night.

Sometimes if I'm feeling down or in an irritable mood, I'm not the least willing. And I can rationalise lots of reasons why I deserve the right to be down, but it doesn't help! I've needed to work through some heavy issues and I'm not finished yet, but if I take these attitudes and hurts to my Lord when I first realise I'm struggling, it takes a

My Rights? My God?

lot less time to work through it.

Sometimes I ask to see his perspective, or at least to have a glimpse of it. Sometimes I ask him to help me focus on things I have to be thankful for in the past. Sometimes I ask him to help me see the humour in situations and be able to laugh. Then sometimes I need him to forgive me for an unkind attitude. Overall, I'm learning to be content, and to be thankful for every day.

Paul tells the Philippians that they have been *given* the privilege of suffering on behalf of Christ. ('It has been *granted* to you on behalf of Christ not only to believe on him but also to suffer for him.' Philippians 1:29) I'm still working on the fact that I've been *given* this wheelchair. My prayer is that through this chair I'll bring glory to God.

Brian and Ruth Clark served with SIM in Liberia for six years and then in Ethiopia for six years. Since 1996 they have been attached to the SIM-USA office.

▶ Chapter 6

Such dangerous places!

The stories you have just read are fortunately very unusual. The ordeals described were deep personal tragedies. We don't include them because you will have similar experiences: you most probably won't. They are here because they're true. They are part of the whole picture. Such things do happen, and they can happen to God's people.

Of course, they happen in our home countries, too. Every day we read of violence and of crippling and fatal accidents. To have a balanced view of life and its risks we need to remember that. But there is no doubt that these things happen more often in the developing countries. If you stay at home you can't be sure of escaping accidents, disease or violence; but if you're called to live in one of the developing countries you do increase your risks. But, I say again, remember that these tragic incidents are unusual; we shouldn't become paralysed by fear.

I believe we all need to prepare ourselves, mentally and spiritually, for the uncertainties of the future. In his first letter, the apostle Peter tells his readers to prepare their

> We all need to prepare ourselves, mentally and spiritually, for the uncertainties of the future

minds for action (1 Peter 1:13). He's describing something that's done ahead of time, not when the crisis has arrived. If that's not done, then when the heat is on, even the truths that will most help us can seem like hollow clichés. Paul's picture of the Christian's armour, in Ephesians chapter 6, teaches us a similar lesson. Half of the pieces of armour he describes are what the soldier will put on in the camp before the battle, not when the enemy is rushing at him! With that picture of the armour as a starter, let's explore what else we should hang around the gallery of our minds to reflect on.

Not just numbers

We've been using words like 'unusual', 'probably', and 'risk'. Those words have their value but they shouldn't make this discussion sound like a statistical exercise. We are not mere statistics, but children of a heavenly Father, the one who is on the throne of the universe. If unwelcome things do happen to us, it's not because we're merely the victims of probability theory. Thank God for that! No, they come from the mystery of God's plan, a plan that flows from his wisdom, love and power. There are no accidents for his children. As Michael Griffiths said in his address at the Memorial Service for the missionaries killed in a road accident in Thailand in 1978 (see below), 'With God there are mysteries, *but no mistakes*'.

> With God there are mysteries, but no mistakes

When we hear of disasters in countries which are known for risk, we often think of those caught up in them as mere statistics. If we hear floods have made 200,000 people homeless, we may do no more than register a six-figure number. But each one of those people is the object of God's love. He is the God who doesn't forget even one sparrow (Luke 12:6). Those thousands are known to God individually. They are people whom he made in his image. But for expatriate Christians

My Rights? My God?

who live in those places, the perspective is very different. They identify with their neighbours and those with whom they work; they enjoy friendship with them.

Good out of evil

When we, too, experience difficulties and tragedies, it can have huge effects on how we are perceived by nationals. Some years ago a mission working in Zambia went through an extraordinary series of tragedies in quite a short space of time. This included several deaths in missionary families. The Zambians were used to having missionaries enter into their sorrows and attend their funerals. The missionaries, on the other hand, tended to return to their home countries when they retired. So when they died (usually some years later) they were buried at home, far from those they worked amongst. Now for the first time, the roles were reversed. The Zambians were attending Westerners' funerals, and sharing their griefs. The deepened bonds that grew out of that experience did more for the work than words could express.

So, too, some fruit has been seen from the tragedy in Manorom, Thailand. On a January day in 1978, a minibus full of missionary families from OMF's Manorom Christian Hospital was returning from an outing. A heavy truck coming towards them pulled out in their path from behind a bus, and in the head-on collision that followed five missionaries, seven of their children, and three unborn babies were killed outright. Why did it happen? On the twentieth anniversary of the event, David Pickard, OMF's General Director, wrote: 'From a less clouded perspective, we can see that God did more that day, and since, than we could have imagined. The Lord promised that we will bear much fruit, and fruit that will last. He never specified how. We have been permitted to see some fruit from the accident in our lifetime. Much will only come to light when we get to heaven.'

He adds that he has met dozens of men and women, from all over the world, whom God changed through hearing about the accident. An

> Much will only come to light when we get to heaven

Australian doctor who lost a child in the crash wrote the following month: 'Manorom, which is known as a very hard place in its reaction to the gospel message, has softened in a way that is hardly believable. At a memorial service on the Tuesday after the accident, hundreds of market people and government officials sat and listened intently to the message of hope.'

A New Zealand surgeon on duty that day had waved off his wife and three children in the morning. Only his son survived. On hearing that his wife and daughters had been killed on impact, he had to set about operating

> God does not have to justify to me, or give his reasons for, what he has permitted

on the survivors. He reflected, 'God does not have to justify to me, or give his reasons for, what he has permitted.' That is true, and came from a profound acceptance that God is God. Yet in his

kindness the Lord does often lift a corner of the curtain to let us see something of the good he plans to bring.

Christ's suffering

Perhaps the biblical theme that can best prepare us for the possibility of hardships is the suffering of Christ. Looking way back into the Old Testament, we find that one of the roles marked out for the Messiah who was to come is that of a servant. It is one of the great themes of the latter part of the book of Isaiah. And if one asks, 'What *kind* of servant is he?' the answer is clear. He is pre-eminently the *suffering* servant. 'His appearance was so disfigured beyond that of any man and his form marred beyond human likeness' (Isaiah 52:14). 'A man of sorrows, and familiar with suffering' (Isaiah 53:3). Store this picture in

My Rights? My God?

your mind, so that you think of it again when the going gets rough.

That wonderful passage in Isaiah takes it further. It was not just that he suffered, but that his sufferings should have been ours: he takes them in our place. 'He was pierced for our transgressions, he was crushed for our iniquities. The LORD has laid on him the iniquity of us all' (Isaiah 53:5,6). Perhaps we should add that aspect to our mental foundation-laying. We are responsible for that suffering; it is not something we can view objectively; and it is the only basis for our spiritual healing.

We are responsible for Christ's suffering

The apostle Peter quotes this passage from Isaiah in his first letter, and in the process he gives us one of the Bible's great explanations of Jesus' death (1 Peter 2:21-25). But what is so striking is that he is applying Jesus' death, and Isaiah's predictions of his sufferings, to encourage those who were suffering. At this point he is writing particularly to slaves who were being treated harshly by their masters (v 18), and we can imagine that that was no picnic! He sympathises with them in their hardships, but urges them to respond with willing service and without retaliation. And to help them in that he points them to the example of Jesus. So we can put it to the same use, as we need it.

Identifying with Christ in his sufferings

We have seen how, in his suffering, Christ identifies with us and dies in our place. He dies that we might not suffer the ultimate suffering – that of hell. But as Paul thinks about the sufferings of God's people, he builds in this thought: we can identify with Christ in *his* sufferings! He picks up this theme when he writes to the Colossian Christians: 'I rejoice in what was suffered for you, and I fill up in my flesh what is still lacking in regard to Christ's afflictions, for the sake of his body, which is the Church' (Colossians 1:24). In this difficult passage, Paul is not teaching that he shares in Christ's bearing our sins. Rather, he sees the Church as bearing a burden of suffering in this world. And as the Church is Christ's body, he sees the Church's suffering as Christ's suffering. Paul counts it a privilege to take his share of that suffering – to contribute towards its completion.

> Paul sees the Church as bearing a burden of suffering in this world

Turning back now to Philippians chapter 3, we feel ourselves responding just as Janet did. We meet in that wonderful passage words which at first we wish Paul had not included. In verse 10 he expresses his highest and deepest aspiration: 'I want to know Christ and the power of his resurrection'. We warm to the challenge of having the same ambition. But then he adds: 'and the fellowship of his sufferings, becoming like him in his death'. Immediately we feel out of our depth. How can we *desire* that? Perhaps our difficulty is because we haven't seen that the last phrase is inseparable from the first. Elsewhere Paul writes that 'everyone who wants to live a godly life in Christ Jesus will be persecuted' (2 Timothy 3:12). It is suffering for Christ's sake that Paul has in mind, and his words reflect that the more we 'know' Christ, and the more we 'want to live a godly life in Christ Jesus', the more we will want the whole package – including the suffering.

Perhaps this theme, more than most, reinforces Peter's plea to prepare our minds. It would be very hard to apply these things to our circumstances if we start to wrestle with them when the battle is already on and we are facing extreme hardships. We need to be laying these foundations *now*, building them into the way we think, and then they will come more readily to mind when we need

My Rights? My God?

The theme of suffering and glory is an intrinsic part of the gospel

them. The theme of suffering and glory is an intrinsic part of the gospel. To change the metaphor again, it is worth setting aside time to mine its rich depths.

Suffering and evangelism

In 1999 Jorge Atiencia, an Ecuadorean who has worked amongst students in IFES movements in South America for thirty years, was expounding 1 Peter to a major European youth missions conference. He noted how the themes of suffering and witness, that is the Christian's response to suffering and its effect on the persecutors, are interwoven in the letter, and he left us with this thought: 'How can our suffering be an evangelistic tool?' What a picture to store in our minds! Here is a call not to withdraw from the battle when we are wounded but to see how our hardships could *advance* the gospel. It happened in the early Church. It has happened repeatedly through the history of the Church. It is happening today.

How can our suffering be an evangelistic tool?

We turn to the Manorom tragedy again for a striking example. Adele Juzi's five-year-old son, Lukas, had been on the outing. She jumped into her car as soon as she heard of the accident, and drove to the scene. There she learned of the death of the twelve, who included Lukas. She writes:

> As I looked at the Thai people gathered round, my heart was filled with pity for them. I prayed, and turning to them I said, 'These people who have died are not here any more. They are already with the Lord, and they were ready to meet him. I have one wish – that you, all of you, will never forget this sad scene, and that whenever you hear anything about the Lord Jesus you will open your

Such dangerous places!

hearts to him, so that when you too have to die you will be as ready to meet the Lord as these people have been.'

The fruit of the Spirit is... joy

Again and again, when you meet Christians who have suffered severely, the difference between the Christian life and stoicism stands out. There is no situation in which the Spirit cannot produce his fruit, and part of that fruit is joy. Incredible though it may seem to others, Christians can know joy even in suffering. Perhaps not easily, but really.

> Christians can know joy even in suffering. Perhaps not easily, but really

I recall hearing this account of one woman's experience. Soon after she became a Christian, there began a period when she moved from one tragedy or hardship to another, in her own life or her family's. The whole story was so grim one could have forgiven her for thinking God had forsaken her. But as she recounted the story, her final words were, 'The wonderful thing is that in all this God never let me down!' Janet and David and Brian and Ruth would say the same. They have proved God in painful and exacting experiences. They need to be heard.

I close this chapter with a quote from Joni Eareckson-Tada. She was paralysed from the neck downwards in a diving accident while still at High School. This intelligent, athletic, artistic teenager suddenly found herself in a wheelchair for the rest of her life. She, like Ruth, has come to terms with the fact that God has *given* her this wheelchair. In a Foreword to a book on healing she reflects:

I have been in a wheelchair now for over three decades, and, thankfully, have found a deeper healing that

My Rights? My God?

satisfies: profound peace, a settled soul, strengthened faith, and a lively, buoyant hope of heaven.[1]

Recommended reading

Eileen Gordon-Smith, *In His Time* (OMF/Christina)
Melvin Tinker, *Why Do Bad Things Happen to Good People?* (Christian Focus Publications)
Henry Frost, *Miraculous Healing: A Personal Testimony and Biblical Study* (OMF/Christian Focus Publications)
Lesley Bilinda, *Colour of Darkness: Rwanda* (Hodder Headline)

Notes

1. Joni Eareckson-Tada, *Miraculous Healing* (Christian Focus/OMF)

My thoughts

My Rights? My God?

Sarah's story

Sarah works in central Asia among the Tibetan Buddhists, a group that few people know much about. She had hoped other Christians from her country might join her, but nobody did, so she went alone. She has made her home in a village on the edge of the grasslands where nomads roam, and she is the only foreigner in the area. It is a four-hour journey by bus from any other English-speaking people, and from any Christian fellowship.

She teaches in a school with around 60 children and five other staff, one of whom gets drunk regularly. The cook's husband beats the children, as does one of the teachers if they don't learn fast enough. A lonely woman leans on her for support and friendship, and makes demands on her when her energy is gone and she is weary.

The school day starts at 6.00am with physical exercises. She doesn't need to take part, but daily living is time-consuming, and this is the cue to light the burner to cook breakfast. The cow dung eventually smoulders into flame. If it is in short supply, sheep manure has to be used instead, which isn't nearly so effective, and can easily slip through the grate.

The school is meant to have a supply of electricity in the evening, but this is erratic. A nearby spring supplies freezing cold water for washing and drinking. It's hardly surprising that none of the children or staff wash either their clothes or themselves for months at a time. Nor that the children's hair is infested with lice.

By 7.00am students call at her door for help with their lessons. Then she teaches a class, and after that a stream of staff and other visitors come and go. Every day is the same, with no privacy, from 7.00am to 10.00pm with no rest. Students and staff all live on the school grounds, which are barely bigger than a football pitch.

Sarah asks her friends to pray for her attitudes. In such a small community, the adults pass their time in gossip and criticism. How can she keep out of it? She finds herself being resentful that her time and her possessions are all public property.

Christians working in the nearest city go out to visit Sarah as often as they can, and take her fresh vegetables to augment her diet. She still hopes others may come to join her in her ministry some time. It's a long-term work and a costly one. Sarah moved thousands of miles away from her family and her boyfriend to settle among these people, and bring them, in the words of the apostle Paul, 'the sweet savour of Christ'. As with others in this book, she felt 'the love of Christ left her no choice'.

Sarah is an Interserve partner. (Her name has been changed as she works in a sensitive area of Asia.)

My Rights? My God?

A letter from Mongolia

Andrew and Jean are part of a team working for Mongolia's development. This letter came shortly after they reached their new home. The climate is inhospitable; temperatures range from -40C to +40C.

After two long months our crate finally arrived. No Christmas boxes have ever been so exciting. Now we have all the clothes, bedding and other items we need to cope with a Mongolian winter. Our petrol stove and tilley lamp have proved invaluable, but fuel is extremely hard to come by.

We began our time here with no electricity, an erratic water supply, and no heating. We are grateful that the Language Institute we work with has provided us with a small generator that can power the twin-tub washing machine. We now have a fairly regular water supply and heating. Today we also had hot water for the first time. We all enjoyed hot baths, but left worse tide marks than the *Braer* oil tanker which sank off the Scottish coast!

We are stocking up for the winter now that our balcony can double up as a freezer. Last week Andrew came back from market with a 21kg leg of beef on his back. We then spent the evening butchering it on our living room table. It cost about 15p per pound and there is no sign of mad cow disease round here. We are becoming increasingly carnivorous as vegetables have all but disappeared from the shops.

Language lessons have been enjoyable, although we struggle to find time to study. We learned a valuable lesson in pronunciation a while ago – for the first month we'd been proudly announcing in Mongolian that we were 'British birds' rather than 'British people'. This probably explains the puzzled reactions.

Andrew is enjoying the Excel correspondence course for Mongolian English teachers. To help overcome the lack of speaking practice, four-day seminars are held every few months. In addition to this we have started an 'English Club' which meets every week. It helps us to get to know the students and gives them language practice, as well as being good fun. One student, PJ, asked for a copy of our 'favourite book'. Jean has also begun teaching English in a nearby primary school for 40 minutes a day.

Our first visit to a *ger* (a Mongolian tent) was an interesting experience. It is a Mongolian tradition to present first-time visitors with large mounds of *buudz* (greasy meat pies) and salty tea. One-year-old Thomas wolfed them down with great relish. However Andrew, suffering from sickness the previous day, had to force down every mouthful, and only just made it home in time! We continue to meet weekly in the *ger* to look at Mark's Gospel, which is a great joy and privilege.

My Rights? My God?

Towards the end of last month, Rose (now three) fell off a seat onto the hard floorboards and broke her collar bone. Fortunately Jean, who has broken her collar bone twice before, knew what to do. After three weeks she is mending well. She continues to be our extrovert toddler and last week ran up to a little gaggle of children in the post office and asked them to be her friends. Although they didn't understand her, they proceeded to follow her home. We continue to have a trail of children coming to play. Thomas is well and speaks as much Mongolian as he does English!

With love and best wishes
Andrew and Jean

A letter from Mongolia

 Chapter 7

Marriage and family life

For some people, life does not include marriage. And that group is especially significant in the world of mission. But single and married missionaries alike need to make their host country their home country, and to feel at home in their house, apartment or *ger*.

> Missionaries all need to feel at home in their house, apartment or *ger*

So what are some of the costs, for home life, of obeying a call to serve abroad? Let's look first at singleness.

Marriage was God's creation, and is given some prominence from the very beginning. See how the first two chapters of Genesis, which bring out different aspects of creation, both put the spotlight on the creation of the sexes, and their relationships and roles. And when the story begins a downward spiral, in chapter 3, it is again the relationship of the man and the woman that is highlighted.

Marriage is the norm for the human race. It is a gift from God. Most people choose marriage, and many single people are not single by choice. So, if I am single, but would still prefer to be married, how will that be affected by a call to serve God abroad? Most people going abroad long-term have reached their late twenties or early thirties before they go. So, even if they stay at home, the prospects of marriage are, humanly speaking, reduced by that stage.

And how does a move to life in another culture affect the situation? Even in cities the number of compatible people you will meet is almost certainly less than you would meet at home. We find examples of people who have met their life partner while at Bible College or after they arrived in their host country, but they are a minority. So comes the question for the single person: granted that God has made you with a desire for marriage, do you have a right to maximise your chances, to avoid taking a route that is likely to reduce them?

Marriage and singleness – both are gifts

It's time to look again at the biblical perspective on this. We saw above that marriage is a gift. So those who are married should see their marriage as something God has given them. That could lead us to think of singleness as a state of deprivation, and singles as those from whom God has withheld a blessing. Let's turn to 1 Corinthians chapter 7, and discover how Paul sees it. In this long and complicated chapter Paul gives us teaching relating to marriage and singleness. Some of it is difficult to interpret with confidence, and certain verses may have particular application to the Corinthians' circumstances at the time. But some parts are very clear.

So, for example, in verse 7 Paul writes: 'I wish that all men were as I am'. By that he means 'unmarried'. Then he continues: 'But each man has his own gift from God; one has this gift, another has that.' Clearly he sees our state – whether married *or* single – as something God has given us. So singleness, too, is a positive gift and not a condition of deprivation. This reflects the Bible's consistent picture of God as both heavenly Father and sovereign Lord.

Our lives aren't the product of our own choices operating within a world of blind chance. God shapes all the facets of our lives, through his power, wisdom and love. We can sympathise with the person who responded to the idea of singleness as a gift from God with the comment: 'The gift that nobody wants!' It may at times seem an unwelcome gift, but it *is* a gift from a loving Father.

There's another biblical insight into singleness, in the words of Jesus in Matthew 19:3-12. Jesus is teaching about the sanctity of marriage. His high standards prompt the retort from his disciples that if divorce is as hard to get as Jesus was teaching, it might be better not to get married in the first place! Jesus responds by saying that not everyone is called to singleness. But he identifies some groups of people who do remain single. Amongst these he describes those who 'have renounced marriage because of the kingdom of heaven' (v 12, NIV). We have pointed out that many single people would prefer to be married. But Jesus identifies another group, whose singleness is voluntary – for the sake of greater usefulness to God. God may call only a few down that path, but we shouldn't overlook the fact that he does call some.

> Jesus identifies another group, whose singleness is voluntary – for the sake of greater usefulness to God. We shouldn't overlook the fact that he does call some that way

If we are to see both marriage and singleness as gifts from God, then we should expect to see each state as having its own advantages and disadvantages. We might also expect that each would show particular advantages and particular drawbacks when transplanted into another culture.

We've already mentioned the disadvantage for singles in going overseas that this reduces the likelihood of finding a husband or wife. Singleness can be a lonely business, especially when you encounter all sorts of new situations. It is a help to have someone to talk them through with.

An unfamiliar culture can throw up all sorts of tensions for a single person. Many of the cultures in developing countries have more restrictive ideas of acceptable behaviour for single people than we are used to in the comparatively free and easy cultures in the West. They won't just be different; sometimes they will be irritatingly rigid! And to ignore them will, in many cases, be to destroy our usefulness. Using our homes for entertainment can be more difficult. A married couple can easily invite visitors of either sex. The single person won't be free to entertain singles of the opposite sex in their home. Likewise, there will be some pastoral tasks that a single person can't undertake.

Housing, opportunities, friendships

Many agencies working abroad own housing for their workers. It may be a financially sensible arrangement but sometimes it produces friction. This can be true for anyone, but mission housing can be particularly difficult for singles. They are often allocated a house, and may have little or no choice as to who they share the house with. After all, married couples have had the choice of who they are to live with – for the rest of their lives. But the single person may have to share a house with a missionary colleague with whom they have little natural affinity and wouldn't choose to spend a holiday with, let alone a four-year term. But there may be no option, other than to return home, defeated. The only route is for us to accept the situation with good grace. In that process many people have been surprised to discover some wonderful lasting friendships.

My Rights? My God?

There are significant advantages to being single, however. In 1 Corinthians chapter 7, Paul points out that married people have all sorts of distracting cares. Single people have only themselves. This gives them greater freedom and flexibility, for example in the use of their time and energy. It is no surprise, then, that some single people have found themselves in fruitful activities that would be impossible for a married man or woman. I think of Gerry, for example, working amongst nomadic peoples, in a ministry which calls for him to spend a lot of his time on the move, to keep in touch with the people he is trying to reach. Or take the story of Sarah at the beginning of this chapter. We could multiply examples. Not all would be as extreme. Some simply show that a single person can sometimes give themselves to a task with less distraction, and fruit can flow from that.

The friendships that are open to the single person are also a plus. It is sad that today's confused moral values in the West mean there is a danger that people will suspect all same-sex friendships of being lesbian or gay. We need to be alert to that. But there is a richness in the range of pure friendships that a single person can enjoy.

> There is a richness in the range of pure friendships that a single person can enjoy

Family life

The family life of married couples, too, is affected by being suddenly transported into the setting of a foreign culture. Some of the costs have been touched on in other chapters, and the next chapter looks particularly at the costs for our children.

The Christian home and family is a place where outsiders should be welcomed and find blessing. It is not surprising that one of the qualifications for spiritual leaders

Gerry spends a lot of his time on the move.

in the New Testament churches is hospitality. But the family also needs time when they are together, when the special bonds that we find in families are refreshed and strengthened. Children need time with parents; husbands and wives need time for and from each other. In our home cultures these things are taken for granted and, if they don't happen, it is in most cases our own fault. Our society leaves us alone. But in many other cultures it is very hard to find ways of shutting the rest of society out of the home for a while. Privacy seems impossible to find. At these times we find ourselves protesting – perhaps only in our own minds – that we are entitled to better than that. We want to claim the right to privacy, but we may have to adapt to the culture and accept that we will have less privacy than we would like. This, too, may be a price we have to pay.

For some parents a major cost lies in exposing themselves and their children to harsh and primitive conditions. Our God-given instinct is to protect our children; it goes deeply against the grain to bring them into hardship. Andrew and Jean, whose story is here, must have felt that keenly when they sensed the Lord calling them to work in Mongolia. At their valedictory service in the UK, both described something of how they sensed God's call. Andrew added that, from the time they were engaged, they began to pray for children who would not only survive, but thrive, in tough conditions. Their commitment to that prayer has been amply tested!

> They began to pray for children who would not only survive, but thrive, in tough conditions

God's companionship

What do we say to all this? I want to pick out just two biblical themes. First, to those who struggle with loneliness in singleness, the Bible presents us with a Father who is concerned for our needs and can help us in them.

So in Psalm 145 David celebrates a God who is our creator, and 'loving towards all he has made' (vv 13,17). We think readily enough of God's wisdom and power being displayed in creation, but the Bible links it with God's compassion and love. Apply this not to people in general, but to yourself, as his beloved child.

In Psalm 146:9, as in other passages, his concern is focused not on the mass of humanity, but on the isolated in particular. He is the God who sustains the fatherless and the widow. And we may surely add 'and the single'. This isn't trivialising the normal role of father or husband but, rather, it asserts that the help and support that God can give are very real. Remember, he is our Creator, and he knows how to help, as no-one else could ever do.

We find this balanced recognition of the natural ways of support and God's ability to replace them in Paul's experience towards the end of his life. In 2 Timothy 4:16 he reveals how much he felt the need of friends to support him, and how deserted he felt when they were not there: 'At my first defence, no-one came to my support, but everyone deserted me'. We sense a note of wistfulness. Here is no super-spiritual denial of his need for human comfort. Then he goes on to say: 'But the Lord stood at my side and gave me strength'. The absence of human friends was a real loss, but God's help was even more real.

> Here is no super-spiritual denial of his need for human comfort

The longing for privacy

And then, to those who chafe at not having a 'proper' home, and who find the loss of privacy hard to take and the intrusion of strangers irksome, let me bring two examples from the life and words of the Lord Jesus Christ. The first is his description of the lifestyle he chose for himself: 'Foxes have holes and birds of the air have nests, but the Son of Man has nowhere to lay his head' (Matthew 8:20). That's a pretty vulnerable lifestyle.

The second example is in his attitude to people – people who could be such a demanding nuisance. Remember how they even pursued him across the lake, when he was looking for a bit of peace and quiet with his friends (Matthew 14:13ff.). Matthew records his response on another occasion: 'When he saw the crowds he had compassion on them, because they were harassed and helpless, like sheep without a shepherd' (Matthew 9:36). He is a hard act to follow. But that is what he calls us to. And where he calls, he also gives the needed grace.

Recommended reading

Albert Y. Hsu, *Singles at the Crossroads: A Fresh Perspective on Christian Singleness* (IVP)

My thoughts

My Rights? My God?

[Scene 1]
Somewhere in Africa.

Little Tim, four years of age, is the oldest child of an Asian father and a British mother, missionaries. Until he goes to school, his only companions are the children of the local church leader. The child closest to Tim in age is an aggressive little boy, and untruthful. Tim learns to lie, too.

His parents are in a dilemma. They know Tim needs other children to play with, but in their home countries he would have the chance to choose his friends. To withdraw him from the company of these children would give him a solitary existence, and carry the real risk of offending the church leader and his wife!

At last it is time for Tim to go to school. Surely this will solve the problems. He is sent to a school for expatriate children in the nearby city. The fees are high, but his parents believe it is worth it. However, there are different problems now.

The school is not primarily for missionary children; most of the pupils are from wealthy expatriate families, enjoying a lifestyle far above that of Tim and his parents. When birthday parties come round, Tim inevitably compares what he sees when he goes to the birthday parties of his new friends with what his parents can manage. That is not easy for Tim or his parents to handle. It obviously troubles him.

After a while the teachers call Tim's parents in and explain that they are concerned about him. He is becoming withdrawn and antisocial. They recommend he be taken to a child psychiatrist. Six months later, things are looking brighter. Tim is happier, and relating better to his peers. That crisis is over.

But life would have been simpler if they had stayed in the UK!

[Scene 2]
In Central Asia.

Marty and Jenny are working in a Central Asian country. The culture has been hardened by decades of harsh totalitarian government. One ugly feature of this is the use of 'shaming' or public humiliation as the normal means of offering correction or reproof – for example in the workplace. This is something of a shock compared with Western (especially North American) cultures, where the prevailing view is that people respond better to encouragement. Marty and Jenny manage to cope with this themselves, but find it very difficult to think of their children having to do so. And it is the primary motivating 'tool' used by the teachers at the school where their two sons attend.

My Rights? My God?

[Scene 3]
Somewhere in Asia.

James moved out to Asia as a toddler, with his British missionary parents. When he reached school age, they were living in a remote village far away from schools, so his mother began home-schooling. Like Tim, above, James' only companions were local children. He quickly picked up their language, and got on well with them. Then friends visiting the home noticed that his behaviour was not developing normally. The cultural gulf between him and his local friends was hampering him. Reluctantly and anxiously, and totally in conflict with what they had planned for their children, his parents accepted that he should go off to the school for missionary children in a neighbouring country.

They shed tears at the parting, but James seemed happy enough, and early reports from the school confirmed that he was well settled. When he came home for the holidays his parents were surprised and delighted at his maturity. When, later, the family returned to the UK for home assignment, relatives remarked on how well he had developed.

Then comes the news that the school at which James had been so happy will be closing. There is no equivalent possibility. His parents feel perplexed as to what to do. They do not want him, or his younger brothers, to be disadvantaged in their education by their parents' missionary call. All over again, James's parents find themselves facing

the battle of 'rights' which they thought was
behind them when they joined the mission. Is it not
their 'right' to give their children the education
of their choice? What are their 'rights' in this
situation?

[Scene 4]
In the UK.

In a public meeting, a young man is describing his
experiences as a child of missionaries in Asia,
with less money than they would have had at home,
disrupted schooling, and all the other things that
go with 'third culture' children's lives.

His uncle had been listening. His own children had
received the best education in the UK that money
could buy. At the end of the meeting the uncle
remarked that their upbringing was comparatively
deprived, alongside the description his nephew had
given of his own childhood! The enrichment of
travel and of different cultures. Firm friendships
with children from several nationalities. Dorm
parents who had put him and his fellow students
first, who had helped them with their homework,
been there at the football games, and encouraged
them in their spiritual lives too. And because he
was away at school, his parents had made sure there
were special times with his family in the holidays.
One thing he had never felt in *any* way was
deprived.

My Rights? My God?

Chapter 8

What do we owe our children?

C hristian parents probably shed more tears and have deeper feelings of failure over their families than over anything else. Children give their parents so much joy, and there is every reason to thank God for them. Yet the task of bringing them up exposes our weaknesses and gives plenty of scope for our sinfulness to find expression.

The family life of people in so-called 'full-time Christian ministry' presents some special problems. That applies to those working in their own culture as well as to those working abroad. And this is especially true for those whose work is partly or largely done from home. There the balance between the demands of ministry and the demands of children becomes particularly hard to get right.

Our temperaments will tend to push us to one extreme or the other. The activist, with very high commitment to the ministry, will be inclined to respond instantly to the call of the work, and leave family responsibilities neglected or even unnoticed. That's a sure formula for creating resentment in the wife or husband, and in the children. No surprise if the children even come to resent their parents' faith which – as they see it – is responsible for

> Our temperaments will tend to push us to one extreme or the other

their neglect. And they may then struggle with inappropriate guilt over that resentment.

Then there's the opposite extreme. We can become so protective of our family and time with them – especially if we are working abroad – that people might well wonder why we are there at all. And our supporters might have the same question! If our sole aim is to care for our family and spend time with our children, we could, after all, do that at home.

Fashions of thinking amongst Christians can swing from one of these extremes to the other. So it's good to know ourselves, and also to recognise what fashion is currently in force!

'Third-culture' children

This is the new term for what used to be called 'missionary kids' or 'MKs'. It's a good one, because children growing up in a host culture, and not the culture of their parents, end up able to live happily in both cultures without feeling that they really belong fully to either. Theirs is a 'third culture'. And there are problems here, as well as privileges. There always will be problems and dangers for families in this fallen world. There is no escaping them, as we all know from our own childhood. But bringing up a family in a foreign culture brings its own share of difficulties.

There are real costs to being a 'third-culture' child. Little Tim's problems may not be unusual. Our Western preoccupation with the nuclear family can lead us to overlook the fact that most human societies make good use of the extended family. Even in our own cultures the extended family plays a more important role than we often realise. So losing that network when we go

Most human societies make good use of the extended family

abroad may be more of a loss than we see at first. Of course, as we make friends in our host country we may find some replacement 'extended family' among them. Now *that* would be enriching to the whole family!

For the first five years of our first child's life, my wife and I lived in a country far from our families, though in a culture which had much in common with our own. We were struck by our daughter's awareness of the fact that her little friends knew their grandparents, uncles and aunts, cousins, while in her case they were no more than names and photographs. How much more significant it is, then, when a child grows up in a very different culture without their extended family.

But let's remember that the best of parenting and the most privileged and sheltered circumstances can never guarantee that a child will 'turn out all right'. Our children share the same fallen humanity that we do, and only God's grace can prevent them making shipwreck of their lives. So avoiding a call to serve in another culture won't guarantee a happy or successful family.

As throughout this book, we want to be realistic about the costs of going abroad. So let's look at some of the problem areas. But as we do so, let us not overlook the compensations and advantages. I hope we'll see both sides.

Education

The problems of schooling must rank high in importance for any parent bringing up children in a foreign country. People living in a city in a 'developed' country may find the facilities so good, and so accessible, that they are not conscious of any drawbacks. But things can be very different in less developed areas. Many missionaries are a long way from a school of any description, and cut off from other expatriate families.

Most people today are fortunate in having a choice of several options for their children. Each of these has its passionate devotees who are sometimes dismissive of all other methods. Often, some painful experience brings us to see that the issues are not as clear-cut as we thought, and we are thankful to have access to an option we had previously dismissed. Sometimes the best use of gifts or resources, or the interests of the mission, can point to an option that would not be our first choice.

Take, for example, a situation where there are two families in the same village. One family prefers home schooling, which would be carried out by the mother. The other family would rather have a trained teacher provided, so that the parents can both give more time to mission activities. That teacher could easily handle teaching the children from both families, and the mission leaders see that that would be the best use of resources. What should the first family do? How do 'rights' come into this?

So whatever our own views are, it's best to avoid dogmatism. In particular it's unwise to ascribe any particular family's problem to their views on children's education. Issues, personalities and circumstances in the real world are too complex for

> Whatever our own views are, it's best to avoid dogmatism

that. We may have all the right theories and practices, but we will still be vulnerable, in this area as we are in others. As the apostle Paul cautions us, 'If you think you are standing firm, be careful that you don't fall!' (1 Corinthians 10:13)

Social development

Both Tim and James are examples of children struggling in their social development as they grow up in a foreign culture. Sometimes the effects are less obvious and less serious. Some problems disappear rapidly when the

Education options

o **National/local school in host country**

o **International day school (where available)**

o **Christian boarding school in host/neighbouring country**

o **Home schooling**

o **Boarding school in home country**

o **Day school in home country**

child returns to more familiar circumstances; for other children the effects go deeper.

We need a sense of perspective about this, as on other points. Many children in our home countries suffer in their childhood development. Through tension in the home, bullying at school, or from many other causes, children suffer and are damaged. As we have noted already, the problems are not limited to those who live abroad. And the quality of home life is of supreme importance for our children's wellbeing, wherever we may be living. Many 'third-culture' children thrive on their childhood circumstances and develop and mature through them.

> The quality of home life is of supreme importance for our children's wellbeing, wherever we may be living

Health and safety

In the minds of many people in the West, accidents and disease form part of the general picture of developing countries. And, as we saw in an earlier chapter,

My Rights? My God?

that image is not without foundation. Missionaries' children do die of malaria. Some are killed in car accidents. Although children die of disease and accidents in our home countries, the risks are greater in developing countries.

On the other hand, life in many of these places is healthier than we imagine. I remember interviewing a young couple who believed they were called to work in Africa. I noted how the wife abhorred spiders, and observed her almost pathological concern for the cleanliness of their little toddler! I said to myself they would never make it. However they were convinced of God's call. And I was wrong. My next mental image of them is from a visit I made to the family two years later. Their daughter, now running around, appeared to spend more time eating with the neighbouring African family than with her own, as they all sat on the ground around their communal cooking pot. Her mother was quite unconcerned. And the child was a picture of robust good health!

The point is that we so easily get these things out of perspective. Yes, there are degrees of risk, but they are just that: they are degrees; they are relative.

* * *

So where is our responsibility in these things? Should we above all else protect our children in a safe environment, and give them the best education? If this is our conclusion, then we should stay at home. Yet we are ignoring the gospel reasons for going. And we are also ignoring the fact that there is no sure way of avoiding all risk while we are in this world. On top of this, we are discounting the significant benefits that our children can gain through the experience.

What had kept James' parents from coming home when their anxieties about his progress, and other

hardships, were at their greatest? I asked them. His father thought for a moment. 'We've always been absolutely sure that God had called us to serve abroad,' he replied, 'and I didn't want to be looking back in thirty years' time, regretting what might have been.'

The compensations

The third and fourth scenes at the beginning of this chapter remind us that there is something else to put in the scales as we weigh up the costs. There are many compensations. Most missionary children find themselves greatly enriched by their upbringing. They experience strange places and cultures; they meet people of many nationalities; they learn other languages; they are enriched by the friendship and example of Christian workers they meet.

Of course, there are casualties, as there are amongst children growing up in their parents' home cultures. But most will be the richer for their experiences. The mission community as a whole shows immense concern for the welfare of our children, and invests a vast amount in research into the issue and providing resources to meet their needs. One survey showed that most 'third culture' children wouldn't hesitate to expose their own children to the upbringing which they themselves had experienced.[1]

Being a Christian parent

Whole books are written on this, of course, and a few paragraphs can't cover the subject. But we have referred to the importance of home life in supporting our children through difficult times, and we should go back to that.

The experience of Marty and Jenny and their family (Scene 2) underlines how important loving support is to our children when we are in a strange culture. Marty and Jenny need to be countering the corrosive effects of that 'shaming' by unmistakable love and acceptance in the home. Even in less extreme circumstances, children are sustained by the confidence they have in their parents' love and acceptance.

> **Children are sustained by the confidence they have in their parents' love and acceptance**

A missionary wife and mother wrote this while looking back on her own experience in a boarding school for MKs:

> It wasn't until my final year as a senior that I realised what a special heritage I had. I felt close to my parents and knew we had a good, honest relationship, but I took it for granted. It wasn't until one of my classmates opened my eyes to what others felt about the relationship they had with their parents that I understood how fortunate I was. 'Marilyn, your parents really love you, don't they?' my friend asked me one day in one of her more pensive moments. 'Sure they do,' I replied, wondering why she even bothered to bring up the subject. 'Well, I don't think mine love me as much,' she said quietly.[2]

Wise parental love will be sensitive to the differences that can exist between children in the same family. The same missionary describes how she thrived on life in a MK school but her younger sister went through a deep crisis. Their parents needed to be alert to the fact that the two sisters had different personalities and had different needs.

Let's turn now to just a few of the biblical guidelines for parents. In Ephesians chapter 6 Paul gives his familiar instruction to fathers to bring their children up 'in the training and instruction of the Lord'. But he adds the thought-provoking command not to 'exasperate' their children! Perhaps parents need to reflect on ways in which they might be 'exasperating' their children. John Stott

My Rights? My God?

expounds that word as making irritating or unreasonable demands, showing harshness and cruelty, humiliating or suppressing them, or showing sarcasm and ridicule.[3] In the parallel passage in Colossians chapter 3, Paul urges fathers, 'Do not embitter your children, or they will become discouraged'.

In 1 Thessalonians chapter 2, Paul describes his relationship to the Thessalonian believers as 'like a mother' (v 7) and 'like a father' (v 11). In so doing he shows us what he thinks mothers and fathers should be like. So the mother is 'gentle… caring for her little children'. The father, in turn, is described as 'encouraging, comforting'.

In all of these passages Paul outlines for us a parental character which would support our children through all kinds of hardships. Many missionaries are natural leaders, and those who lead instinctively may need to take special note of this. Their strength of character can often bypass the gentle encouragement that a child may be urgently needing.

The grace of God

Parents have a deep desire to protect their children and do what is best for them. And we can be very sensitive to the accusation that we are requiring sacrifice of our children for the sake of our own call.

Let's close the chapter with two thoughts about the character of God. First, our God acts graciously – with mercy and compassion. He created parenthood and the family: they are his idea. He is the God who created parental love: he understands it better than we do. So when he calls us to a path that may include some hardship

> He created parenthood and the family: they are his idea. He is the God who created parental love

not only for us but for our children, he does it as that kind of God: our gracious Father.

And the second thought is this: God's grace is undeserved. Whatever he calls us to, and whatever he brings into our lives, the good is more than we deserve, and the hardships are less. In his books the balance is always heavily on that side. He is no man's debtor. As the old hymn has it: 'he giveth and giveth and giveth again.'

Recommended reading

Marion Knell, *Families on the Move* (Monarch)
Marylin Schlitt, *Deprived or Privileged?* (OMF)

Notes

1. See M H Taylor, 'Personality Development in the Children of Missionary Parents' in *Helping Missionaries Grow: Readings in Mental Health and Development* (William Carey Library, Pasadena).
2. Marilyn Schlitt, *Deprived or Privileged?* (OMF), p 48.
3. John Stott and J. Alec Motyer (eds), *The Message of Ephesians* (IVP), p 246.

My Rights? My God?

My thoughts

What do we owe our children?

He had no rights

He had no rights:

No right to a soft bed, and good food on the
   table;
No right to a home of his own, a place where he
   could relax;
No right to choose good-humoured friends, who could
   understand him and be there for him;
No right to shrink away from filth and sin, to
   pull his clothes closer around him and turn away
   to walk in nicer places;
No right to be understood and appreciated; no, not
   by those he loved best;
No right not to be forsaken by his Father, who
   meant more than anything to him.

His only right was silently to endure shame,
   spitting blows; to take his place as a sinner at
   the dock; to bear my sins in anguish on the
   cross.

He had no rights. And I?

A right to the comforts of life? No, but a right
   to the love of God for my pillow.
A right to physical safety? No, but a right to the
   security of being in his will.
A right to love and sympathy from those around me?
   No, but a right to the friendship of the one who
   understands me better than I do myself.

A right to be a leader? No, but the right to be
   led by the one to whom I have given everything,
   led as a little child, with its hand in the hand
   of its father.
A right to a home and dear ones? No, not
   necessarily; but a right to dwell in the heart
   of God.
A right to myself? No. But I do have a right to
   Christ.

All that he takes I will give;
All that he gives I will take;
He is my only right!
Everything else fades away before him.
I have full right to him;
May he have full right to me!

*This is the closing chapter (slightly edited) of
Mabel Williamson's book 'Have we no rights?'*

▶ Chapter 9

Christ with us

W e've nearly done. It's time to reflect, and draw to a close. We've looked at some of the implications of responding to a call to serve God abroad. Along the way we've reminded ourselves of the overall reasons for going – to bring the gospel to a world that desperately needs to hear it. We've seen there are some real costs and real rewards. We've learned from the experiences of those already there. In this last chapter we'll spend a little more time going over some of the biblical themes that can help us in the stock-taking, cost-counting process. We'll choose four that focus on Christ. The first two present us with a high call; the second two lead us to ways in which God gently helps us to respond to that call.

> There are some real costs and real rewards

The Lord to be obeyed

People of our generation assert their autonomy. They are their own people, and resent authority. This way of thinking is part of the air we breathe in our Western cultures, and it can seep into our attitudes. It can touch even our relationship with God. Our God is Lord and King! Yes, he is kind and compassionate. Yes, he is gracious and forgiving. But he is also Lord! And Christ shares that lordship. The corollary of that is, as Paul puts it: 'You are not your own; you were bought at a price' – the price of Christ's death for us (1 Corinthians 6:19,20). Jesus is Lord. He is our king. He has absolute right to plan and shape our lives, because we belong to him. We are his because he made us, and his because he bought us.

Earlier in the book we looked at one biblical picture of this – that of the potter. Listen to the words of Isaiah chapter 45: 'Woe to him who quarrels with his Maker, to him who is but a potsherd among the potsherds on the ground. Does the clay say to the potter, "What are you making?"' (v 9). As he calls us to follow him, Jesus tells us that his yoke is easy (Matthew 11:30). The whole passage (vv 28-30) is full of gentle encouragement. But note that Jesus doesn't say that there is no yoke! There is still a yoke, and a yoke serves to guide the ox where the farmer wants him to go! We are to be at his disposal, and to go where he directs. But that bondage is true freedom; that death is true life.

We are to be at his disposal, and to go where he directs.

The Example to be followed

Examples are there to be followed. An example does two things. It shows that something *can* be done; it takes an action from the realm of theory into the world of practice. And an example also shows us *how* it can be done. Jesus is a model for us in both of these ways. So when he calls us to any path of costly obedience, we know this: he is not sending us on some impossible journey, far removed from our world. No, he has walked that path himself. And as we watch him, through the pages of the Bible, we can see how to walk that path ourselves.

One of the most wonderful biblical pictures of Jesus as the 'servant-king' is found in Philippians 2:6-8.

> ... Christ Jesus: who, being in very nature God, did not consider equality with God something to be grasped, but made himself nothing, taking the very nature of a servant, being made in human likeness. And being found in appearance as a man, he humbled himself and became obedient to death – even death on a cross!

He was not compelled to come. He had a full right to hold on to all the expressions of his deity. He could have stayed in heaven and avoided all the many features of humanity that were part of his becoming man. But he did not consider that 'something to be grasped'; he surrendered it for us. And Paul brings us these thoughts not only as profound theology, but also quite explicitly as an example for us to follow. Note how he begins this section: 'Your attitude should be the same as that of Christ Jesus'.

The Companion who strengthens us

At the end of Matthew's gospel, we find what we often call the 'Great Commission' (Matthew 28:18-20). Here Jesus bids his apostles farewell and sends them off on their life's work. As part of that he gives them this promise: 'Surely I am with you always, to the very end of the age.' I think we can easily miss what a profound thing this is. It can seem almost trivial. So it is striking that that simple promise accompanies the great things they are taught ('all authority is given to me') and the great things they are to be doing (preaching, teaching, baptising).

One of the effects of suffering and hardship is to make us feel isolated. Peter recognises this when he tells suffering Christians that their sufferings are the same as those being experienced by others (1 Peter 5:9). It should be a great comfort and encouragement to know that we are never alone. Christ is with us. Two incidents in the life of Paul give us examples of this. During his first missionary travels in Greece, his message was largely rejected in Athens and also (to begin with) in Corinth, the next place on his route. Then one night, in Corinth, the Lord spoke to him in a vision: 'Do not be afraid; keep on speaking, do not be silent. For *I am with you*' (Acts 18:9,10). That was the answer to his fears and doubts: Christ was with him. And as we have already seen, the same happened again very near the end of Paul's life, when he was on trial. At that point of great vulnerability, when he felt deserted by his friends, he writes that 'the Lord stood at my side and gave me strength' (2 Timothy 4:17).

The Compensator for our losses

More than once, and in very strong terms, Jesus warns his followers that being a disciple could be a costly business. But at the same time he promises them rich compensation. Listen, for example, to this: '"I tell you the truth," Jesus said to them, "no-one who has left home or wife or brothers or parents or children for the sake of the kingdom of God will fail to receive many times as much in this age and, in the age to come, eternal life"' (Luke 18:29,30).

Could that really be true? Does it sound a bit glib? He is talking about serious losses – home, wife, children… And his hearers knew that the possible losses were real. This was no airy-fairy stuff. How can we understand his promises, then? It's clear that the 'many times as much' compensation isn't literal. But can it be real? And in this life as well as the next? Yes, it can!

In the opening chapter of this book, I said I wanted to maintain the right balance between presenting

My Rights? My God?

the reality of hardships on the one hand, and the rich compensations on the other. In talking about these things with many people, two conversations stand out. Both were with experienced missionaries who had suffered real hardships. Both of them urged me not to overlook the compensations! That simply confirms the impression I have gained through friendships with many missionaries: they are generally a positive, happy group of people! They have found Christ to be a loving and generous taskmaster. He is a rich compensator.

Counting the cost

If I accept his high call, with its costs, might the 'bottom line' end up 'in the red', with a cost that outweighs the benefits? Never! 'God is no-one's debtor.' That bottom line will always be in the black.

Turn again with me to the New Testament, to Luke 14:25-33. Jesus is telling his hearers that serving him must overshadow all other commitments. He introduces two parables, both of which teach the folly of making an important decision without weighing up the pros and cons. Of course, he has in mind our decision to follow him. He doesn't want followers who rush unthinkingly into discipleship. In one story, he talks of starting a building project without calculating the costs properly; in the other he uses the illustration of a king going to war without assessing his own forces, and those of the enemy.

Do Jesus' stories imply that someone might quite reasonably come to a different conclusion? Is it conceivable that following him might *not* be worth the cost? No way! If we do the sums right, there is never any doubt about the bottom line.

Jesus is calling us to full-blooded discipleship. Are you ready for that? Would you really settle for anything less?

My thoughts

My Rights? My God?

Further reading

Operation World: The Day-by-Day Guide to Praying for the World, Patrick
    Johnstone (ed) (OM Publishing)
Christian Ministry Sourcebook, Stephen Froom (Genesis Publications Inc.)
The Contemporary Christian: Applying God's Word to Today's World,
    John Stott (IVP)
Desiring God: Meditations of a Christian Hedonist, John Piper (IVP)
Faithful Witness: The Life and Ministry of William Carey, Timothy George
    (IVP)
God can be trusted, Elizabeth Goldsmith (OM Publishing)
God's Mission and ours: the challenge of telling the nations, Peter T.
    O'Brien (ed) (Good Book Company)
Killing Fields, Living Fields, Don Cormack (OMF/Monarch)
A Mind for Missions: Ten Ways to Build Your World Vision, Paul Borthwick
    (Navpress)
Mind the Gap, Cathie Bartlam (ed) (Scripture Union)
Any biography of Hudson Taylor (several available published by CLC,
    OMF, Bethany, Christian Focus Publications)

Further action

Listen to the CD, then turn to the Appendices and boot up your
computer!

Thanks
The publishers are indebted to FEBA/FEBC for creating the attached CD,
and in particular to its Producer, David Miller. We would like to express
our thanks to all the artists who have given permission for their work to
be featured.

▶ Appendix 1:
Who Works Where

Some societies work in one geographic region, or with certain people groups. Others work globally. This book is published by OMF International and SIM. OMF works in East Asia and among East Asian peoples around the world; SIM works in Africa, South America and Asia. In common with all the societies whose websites are featured here, our first aim is to bring glory to God through the building up of his Church. To that end, we work in partnership with national Christians.

Most mission agencies have a regular magazine or webzine. They also send out news and prayer bulletins for friends and supporters who want to get behind the work by praying. Browse these websites to find out what God is doing around the world, and how you can be part of that.

For a comprehensive list of the major organizations in the USA & Canada consult the Mission Handbook published by EMIS (Evangelism and Missions Information Service). For further information about mission opportunities contact the Website of the Billy Graham Center Library at: www.billygrahamcenter.org.

Society	Web address
Action Partners	www.actionpartners.org.uk
AIM International	www.aim-eur.org
Arab World Ministries	www.awm.org
BMS World Mission	www.bms.org.uk
CLC	www.clc.org.uk
Christian Vocations	www.christianvocations.org
Christian Witness to Israel	www.cwi.org.uk
Church Mission Society	www.cms-uk.org

Crosslinks	www.crosslinks.org
Emmanual International	www.argonet.co.uk/users/emm.int
European Christian Mission	www.ecmi.org
FEBA	www.feba.org.uk
FEBC	www.febc.org.
France Mission Trust	www.france-mission.org
Frontiers	www.frontiers.org
HCJB-UK	www.hcjb.org
IFES	www.ifesworld.org
Interserve	www.interserve.org
ISCS	www.iscs.org.uk
Latin Link	www.LatinLink.org
Leprosy Mission	www.leprosymission.org
Medical Missionary Association	www.healthserve.org
Middle East Christian Outreach	www.gospelcom.net/meco
Novi Most International	www.novimost.org
OMF International	www.omf.org
OMS International	www.omsinternational.org/uk
Operation Mobilisation	www.om.org
Pioneers	www.pioneers.org
Pocket Testament League	www.ptl.org.uk
Qua Iboe Fellowship	http://web.ukonline.co.uk/ qua.iboe/index.htm
Radio Worldwide	ourworld.compuserve.com/ homepages/rw
Red Sea Mission Team	www.rsmt.u-net.com
Servants of Asia's Urban Poor	www.zeta.org.au/~servants/
SAO Cambodia	www.sao-cambodia.org
SIM	www.sim.org
South American Mission Society	ourworld.compuserve.com/ homepages/samsgb
Southern Baptist Convention	www.imb.org
Spanish Gospel Mission	members.aol.com/spngospel
UFM Worldwide	www.ufm.org.uk
WEC International	www.wec-int.org
Wycliffe Bible Translators	www.wycliffe.org.uk
YWAM	www.ywam-england.com

For a full list of evangelical missions with a sending base in your country, contact the following:

AUSTRALIA
Mission Interlink
PO Box 333, Mitcham, Victoria 3132   Phone: 3 9890 0644
www.evangelicalalliance.org.au

HONG KONG
Hong Kong Association of Christian Missions
PO Box 71728, Kowloon CPO   Phone: 2392 8223
www.hkacm.org.hk

MALAYSIA
Malaysian Evangelical Fellowship Missions & Evangelism Commission
PO Box 58, 46700 Petaling Jaya   Phone: 3 735 7328
kohgl@attglobal.net

NETHERLANDS
Eedrachtstraat 29a, 3784 KA Terschuur   Phone: 342 462666
omf_nl@compuserve.com

NEW ZEALAND
Missions Interlink
PO Box 27548, Mt.Roskill, Auckland 1030   Phone: 9 625 0030
missions.jenkins@xtra.co.nz

PHILIPPINES
Philippine Missions Association
PO Box M-006, 1550 Mandaluyong City   Phone: 2 533 6075
pma@jmf.org.ph

SINGAPORE
Singapore Centre for Evangelism & Missions
PO Box 1052, Raffles City, Singapore 9117   Phone: 325 1237
http://scem.antioch.com.sg

SOUTH AFRICA
World Mission Centre
PO Box 36147 Menlo Park, 0102   Phone: 12 343 1165
www.worldmissioncentre.com

UK
Global Connections
Whitefield House, 186 Kennington Park Road, London, SE11 4BT
Phone: 020 7207 2156
www.globalconnections.co.uk

USA
Advancing Churches in Missions Commitment
4201 North Peachtree Road, Suite 300, Atlanta, GA 30341
Phone 770 455 8808
www.acmc.org

Evangelical Fellowship of Mission Agencies
4201 North Peachtree Road, Suite 300, Atlanta, GA 30341
Phone: 770 457 6677
efma1@compuserve.com

Interaction Inc.
PO Box 158, Houghton, NY 14744 Phone: 716 567 8774
www.tckinteract.net

Interdenominational Foreign Mission Association
PO Box 398, Wheaton, Illinois 60189 Phone: 630 682 9270
http://www.ifmamissions.org

My Rights? My God?

▶ Appendix 2: Bible Colleges

The following colleges offer full-time and part-time training courses for cross-cultural mission or for other kinds of long-term biblical ministry. Some also have distance-learning arrangements. This is not an exhaustive list, and it doesn't imply anything about those not featured. For a full list of residential and non-residential colleges, please consult the associations in Appendix 1.

Australia

College	Website
ACOM (Australian College of Ministries)	www.uq.net.au/kcc
Adelaide College of Ministries	http://people.enternet.com.au/~leighr/ACM/home.htm
Bible College of Queensland	www.powerup.com.au\~biblec
Bible College of South Australia	www.biblecollege.sa.edu.au
Bible College of Victoria	www.bcv.aus.net
Harvest Bible College	www.harvestbc.com.au
Moore Theological College	www.moore.edu.au/
Perth Bible College	www.pbc.wa.edu.au
Presbyterian Theological Centre-Sydney	www.presbyterian.org.au/ptcsyd/
Queensland Baptist College of Ministries	www.buq.org.au
Southern Cross College	http://www.southerncross.edu.au
Sydney Missionary & Bible College	www.ozemail.com.au/~smbc
Tabor College	www.tabor.edu.au
WEC Missionary Training College	www.worldview.edu.au
Wesley Institute for Ministry & the Arts	http://www.wesleymission.org.au/centres/wima/default.htm

New Zealand

College	Website
Bible College of New Zealand	www.bcnz.ac.nz
Capernwray Bible College	www.capernwray.co.uk/nz.html
Carey Baptist College	www.carey.ac.nz

Faith Bible College — www.yellowpages.co.nz/for/faithbiblecollege

New Covenant International Bible College — www.ncibc.ac.nz

Pathways College of Bible and Mission — www.pathways.ac.nz

Singapore

Assemblies of God Bible College — http://home1.pacific.net.sg/~bisagbc

Discipleship Training Centre — www.singnet.com.sg/~disciple

Far Eastern Bible College — www.lifefebc.com

Singapore Bible College — http://home1.pacific.net.sg/~sbc1997

Trinity Theological College — www.ttc.edu.sg

Tung Ling Bible College — www.tungling.com

South Africa

Africa School of Mission — www.asm.co.za

Baptist Theological College of South Africa, Cape Town — www.ctbtc.org.za

Baptist Theological College of Southern Africa — www.btc.co.za

Bible Institute-Eastern Cape — www.idesign.co.za/biec

Cornerstone Christian College — www.nis.za/~cornerst

Evangelical Seminary of Southern Africa — www.methbooks.co.za/ebsemsa.html

George Whitefield College — www.gwc.ac.za

United Kingdom

All Nations Christian College — www.allnations.ac.uk

Belfast Bible College — www.bbc-ni.org

Birmingham Bible Institute — www.charis.co.uk/bbi/

Capernwray Bible School — www.capernwray.co.uk

Cliff College — www.cliffcollege.ac.uk

Cornhill Training Course — ctc@proctrust.org.uk

Evangelical Theological College of Wales — www.etcw.ac.uk

Faith Mission Bible College — www.faithmission.org

International Christian College — www.icc.clara.co.uk

London Bible College — www.londonbiblecollege.ac.uk

London Theological Seminary — www.lts.u-net.com

Mattersey Hall — www.matterseyhall.com

Moorlands College — www.moorlands.ac.uk

Nazarene Theological College — www.nazarene.ac.uk

My Rights? My God?

Oak Hill College	www.oakhill.ac.uk
Oxford Centre for Mission Studies	www.icmc.org/ocms
Redcliffe College	www.redcliffe.org
Regents Theological College	www.regents-tc.ac.uk
Southall Sch of Lang & Miss'y Orient'n	www.southallschooloflanguages. sagenet.co.uk
St John's College	www.stjohns-nottm.ac.uk
Spurgeon's College	www.spurgeons.ac.uk
Trinity Theological College	www.trinity-bris.ac.uk
Wycliffe Hall	www.wycliffe.ox.ac.uk

USA & Canada

For a comprehensive list of schools offering programs in missions consult the Directory of Schools and Professors of Mission and Evangelism published by the EMIS (Evangelism and Missions Information Service). For a list of school Websites consult the Directory page on the EMIS Website.

CD Music

Track 1:
* Heavy, © Rob Kirkwood

Track 2:
* *Tunay Nga* (Tagalog, *True For Sure*)
Excerpt, © PAPURI! FEBC Philippines
COMPOSER: JONATHAN MANALO
ARRANGER: MON FAUSTINO
INTERPRETER: MON FAUSTINO
BACK-UP VOCALS & ARRANGEMENT:
MON FAUSTINO
ADDITIONAL BACK-UP VOCALS: JUDITH
BANAL
CO-PRODUCERS: MON FAUSTINO &
JUNGEE MARCELO

Chorus:
You truly are great.
Nobody is greater than You.

Vamp:
You're great, oh God.
Utter praise to You.
Glory to You.

You don't change with time.
You're always there at my side,
Watching, guiding.

Not once You've left me, bless You.
No one is like You.
What can we say greater than You?

Bridge:
Wherever I go, Your love can be
    felt.
Praises and unending thanksgiving
to You, Jesus.

Track 4:
* *Selah I*
Excerpt from Naanu Ninna Daasa
(Kannada, *He's My God & Your
God*), © FEBA-India
MUSICIAN: ROHIT ARASU

Track 5:
* *Bin Yesu Ho Nahin* (Hindi, *Without
Jesus, No Salvation*) Excerpt,
© FEBA-India
SINGER: VINOD VISHVAS

Without Jesus, there is no salvation,
no salvation.
I searched East, West, and all over
the world.
But in the Bible alone I found the
way of truth.

Track 6:
* *Rollicking Flute & Funky Sitar*
Excerpt from Mangala Me Yesu
(Telugu, *Jesus, You Are A Blessing*),
© FEBA-India
MUSICIAN: MR DHAMODARAN

Track 8:
* *Selah II*
Indian folk music. Flute,
tambourine & tabla, a pair of
layered-membrane drums - one
metal and one carved from a block
of hardwood. © FEBA-India

Track 10:
* *Kulintang*
The kulintang is a Philippine
instrument made up of 8 knobbed
gongs, suspended in a wooden
frame.
Excerpt from Sa Dulang ng
Panginoon (Tagalog, *The Lord's
Table*)
© PAPURI! FEBC- Philippines
COMPOSER: PSALMER PAGALAN

My Rights? My God?

Track 11:

* *Ikaw Pala* (Tagalog, *So It's You*)
Excerpt, © PAPURI! FEBC-
Philippines
COMPOSER/LYRICIST: LAARNI MACARAEG
ARRANGER: MARVIN QUERIDO
INTERPRETER: TERRY JAVIER
BACKGROUND VOCALS: RUTH BAGALAY

How I feel light now that You're
in my life.
Whatever trials may come, You're
my support,
A friend I could never forget.

Chorus:
So it's You who gives light & hope.
A smile appears to me, brilliant.
So it's You I needed in answer to
my prayers,
A Guide & Love that has no end.

Bridge:
However often I hurt & forsake
You,
You always intend to forgive.
At any time, it's still You,
Always ready to accept me.
A Guide & Love that has no end.

Track 12:

* *Alleluia Ang Aawitin* (Tagalog,
'Alleluia' Is Our Song) Excerpt
© PAPURI! FEBC- Philippines
COMPOSER: KAHLIL STANLEY REFUERZO
ARRANGER: MARVIN QUERIDO
INTERPRETERS: GERI GATCHALIAN-GIL &
TRICIA AMPER-JIMENEZ
BACK-UP VOCALS: RUTH ROCABO-
BAGALAY, LARRIE ILAGAN, JUNGEE
MARCELO & LANIE ODULIO
BACK-UP VOCAL ARRANGEMENT:
MARVIN QUERIDO

It's been a long search for Your
great purpose,
Ever since our forefathers, until
now.

There's nothing else we can ask,
Oh God, perfect in goodness.
These songs of thanksgiving are
praises to You.

Chorus:
We will sing 'Alleluia' to You,
oh God,
Just for You alone.
We will sing 'Alleluia' to You,
oh God, forever
Because Your faithfulness is truly
great,
Intended without end.

Bridge:
Our praise, oh God, is only for you,
just for you
Because You're great, because
You're great.

Track 13:

* *Yesu Wei No Kidum Nan*
(Malayalam, *Looking Only to Jesus*)
Excerpt © FEBA-India
COMPOSER: MR ISAAC
LYRICS: ISAAC MANOOR
SINGER: MR KESTER

Chorus:
I will look on Jesus as I go through
life's journey
Steadfastly each day I'll go, singing
songs of joy.

Jesus came to this earth to remove
the destructive effects of
sin and its curse
The one who carries the marks of
the nails has delivered me from
sin.

Holding my hand he'll lead me on,
When times of trouble arise
I'll worship and praise him today
and forever. In newness of life, I'll
live for Him.

* **Selah Salita**
Excerpt from Salita Mo Panginoon
(Tagalog, *Your Word, oh God*)
© PAPURI! FEBC- Philippines
COMPOSER: ROBERT DAVID
SINGERS: TERRY JAVIER, CATHY AMACA,
BONG AQUINO, BOBBY BAGALAY

Track 15:
* **Selah III**
Excerpt from En Nangula
Raskshagan Yeshua (Malayalam,
Yeshua, My Blessed Protector)
© FEBA-India
COMPOSER: SARAH NAVROJI

Track 17:
* **Selah IV**
Excerpt from Sa Iyo Lang Aawit ng
Papuri (Tagalog, We Will Sing
Praise Only to You),
© PAPURI! FEBC - Philippines
COMPOSER: JON LICERIO

Track 18:
* **Maaari Naman** (Tagalog, It *Really Is
Possible*) Excerpt
© PAPURI! FEBC - Philippines
COMPOSER: BONG HERMOZA
ARRANGER: MARC LOPEZ
INTERPRETER: CHAI ALEGARBES
BACK-UP VOCALS: RUTH ROCABO-
BAGALAY & LANIE ODULIO
ADDITIONAL VOCALS & ARRANGEMENT:
PRO MC

Yeah man, whatever the situation,
it's really possible.

Vamp:
Come on, let's all move.
Come on, let's all dance.
Come on, let's all shout 'O
Hallelujah!'

Chorus:
It's really possible to move.
It's really possible to dance
'Cause a cheerful heart dances
    automatically.
It's really possible to move.
It's really possible to shout.
In our praising God everyday.

Dance, let's rejoice & clap.
Offer a celebration to Yahweh.

Shout, move, dance.
Join in and shout Hallelujah,
An offering to Yahweh.

CD Music